I've Got Aspergers, so I'm better than you… Shh don't tell mom!

Adam Schwartz

Dedications:

To Sol, Lev and everyone who feels like they don't fit in.

Acknowledgements:

This book would not have been possible without all the good Neurotypicals who helped me write it. I would like to thank Elizabeth Mackling and David Lipnowski with help with the cover. I would also like to thank, Joanne, Eric, Kate, and Jenni-May for being my beta readers.

Finally, none of this would have been possible without the support of my loving parents and the warm embrace of the Winnipeg Stand-up community.

Table of Contents

1. So it Begins

After an open mic comedy set, at the local bar Jekyll and Hyde's, in Osborne Village, Winnipeg Manitoba, two girls approached me. One girl slurred, "Hey that was a really great set. It must be super nerve-wracking standing up there and telling jokes about having Aspergers. Like, at one point you were talking about your difficulties making friends and, like, Sheldon on the Big Bang Theory has, like, no interest in making friends. Also, wouldn't you be more comfortable in, like, a computer lab somewhere than, like, a crowded bar?"

I reassured them I was quite comfortable where I was, but thanked them for their concern.

"Are you sure you have Aspergers then?" She replied. "Because you're not at all like my cousin Mike!"

It is possible that I was little worse tempered than I should have been and that I shouldn't have been as critical of her question. After all, she was just trying to learn about Aspergers and she did not realize that the Autism spectrum is as wide as it is where, like beautiful snowflakes no two people on the spectrum are the same. Some of my comedian friends had already that they had gotten into the Winnipeg Comedy Festival, and I hadn't heard a thing so I replied a bit brusquely. "No. I don't have Aspergers. I am just telling jokes about having Aspergers so you'll sleep with me. You know, because all girls want a guy who understands them slightly less than all the other guys, or stares at their friends' chests, because we can't make eye contact."

2

"Okay, there's no need to be such a grump about it!" she said. "Gawd. I thought you guys were supposed to be always cheerful. " Her friend tugged her arm, and whispered drunkenly to her as they walked away, "People with Aspergers aren't always cheerful." Finally, someone with some sense. "That's people with Downs Syndrome." She did not just say that. I did not just hear that. Neurotypicals are the worst.

There are many ways of separating people; one of the most important is whether someone is on the autism spectrum or not. People on the autism spectrum, or Aspies as we like to call ourselves, occupy the one category, and people not on the spectrum, or Neurotypicals as we like to refer to them, occupy the other. Being an Aspie is difficult, as it often feels like all of society is against us. In addition, it makes every aspect of our lives extra complicated, from making friends, to getting a job, to finding romance. As much as I would love to be a Neurotypical – since it would go great with my otherwise privileged status of being a white middle class male and it would have made life much easier – I am glad I have autism since quite frankly, we are better for it. We don't have the same ridiculous values and we don't care about Kim Kardashian. And we are far enough apart from the norm that we can see just how ridiculous Neurotypicals really are.

If you have Aspergers and go to a party, you are generally not going to be at the center. Instead, you will find a little quiet place in the corner and watch what is going on around you. Sometimes it can be quite funny when everyone except you has been drinking and watching the ridiculous things people do and the ridiculous things people say. Some people, when they're drinking, start thinking that their way is the only way, while other people think they are invulnerable and try to jump off a roof of their friend's garage.

Then there is a much smaller group of people at the party that is really awesome. These people, like my parents and my brother and sister, are warm and generous, and don't take anything for granted. Frankly, I think that the only thing holding these people back from truly being great is that they are Neurotypical.

3

Well, I could go on forever about how awesome this group is, I won't because frankly they are not as interesting or as hilarious as the vast majority who are not as awesome.

I know some people will have a hard time with my generalizing about Neurotypicals but, and this comes from the bottom of my heart, get over it. You have all the privilege and opportunity, heck I am jealous more than half the time at all the things you get to do. In addition, Neurotypicals have been generalizing about us for decades and are even the ones who defined Aspergers in the first place.

After dealing with questions like that of the girl at the bar's a million times, or having to deal with grandparents who are worried that their grandchildren's lives are ruined, or people who see Aspergers as a disability, I have absolutely no problem turning the equation around to point out Neurotypicals are the ones with the problems. Some people even avoid getting their children vaccinations for fear that it may give them Aspergers. They would rather their child catch smallpox, or a million and one other diseases that doctors have worked their whole lives trying to prevent, they would rather risk their children catching life-threatening disorders, and even spread them on to other children, than get their child vaccinated. For the record, vaccinations have been proven not to give children autism, regardless of what Jenny Mccarthy might say, even if she dated a doctor, which would account for any credibility she might think she has, or that anyone credits her with no matter how little credibility that is.

This book is not a science book, therefore I will not be really focusing on this issue any more than in the three sentences above. This is a book about the challenges that people with autism face in relation to neurotypical people's privileged status that for a large part they take for granted. It is also a book that examines how ridiculous neurotypical people truly are, and how people with Aspergers should be thankful that's not us.

Most books about Aspergers do not tell you this truth, but make Aspergers out to be the problem and then try to advice you about getting along in neurotypical society. Well this isn't an advice book for people with Aspergers. I would have to be pretty full of myself to think that I could give any advice to people that I don't know, people who didn't even ask me for advice in the first place. I would have to think that I had the whole thing figured out, which is definitely not the case. After having studied Neurotypicals for the last 28 years, I have still barely scratched the surface and am no expert by any means.

A second reason why I would never give advice is that there is such a wide spectrum of people who have Aspergers that most of the advice anyone can give, no matter how good-hearted their intentions or how knowledgeable they are on the subjects involved, can't satisfy everyone. Things I have read in advice books for people with Aspergers are perfect examples of this phenomenon. Remember to shower every day, especially if you're going to go on a date, and if you don't like to drive, you should make sure when you move that you end up on a bus route that goes past your workplace. Gee whiz! Thank you, Captain Obvious.

I don't know who is buying books written for such a large audience. Their advice would necessarily have to be no more practical than going to see a fortune teller. After all, fortune tellers, through the power of their magic and skill, can tell you that you might have a child, that you might run into someone you haven't seen in a long time, or that your long lost grandfather is trying to communicate with you from beyond the grave. In reality, all they can tell you with certainty is that one day you will die. There's not a huge market for books – or fortune tellers – that give you that information. If this is the best a book can do, no wonder young people are not reading as much as they used to.

The truth is, Neurotypicals belong to a duplicitous, hypocritical group that is as diverse and as strange as we Aspies are, and hopefully by reading this book you will be more aware of some of the challenges we face trying to fit into a neurotypical society and just how crazy some Neurotypicals really are.

2. How I Learned the Rules of Society

Neurotypical people, people without Aspergers are complicated, confusing and extremely frustrating. Yet, since they are the majority, and since we have to interact with them on a daily basis, it is important to try and come up with rules so that you have a chance, however slim, of anticipating what they are going to do next. I mean your family might try to give you some advice for making friends like make sure to shower and use deodorant every day. This is good advice because people hate hanging around other people who smell. On the other hand, it is hardly a step-by-step guide. Therefore, it is a bit like an astronaut visiting another planet they might tell you to keep your helmet which provides the air on, but the rest you have to figure out on your own. There are many ways of studying Neurotypicals, for example, a person can read books, and watch social interactions live as well as on television.

While people watching is a popular past time and people can engage in it in a wide variety of settings such as the mall, the beach, or the park, just to give a few examples, all of these interactions are quite limited. In addition, Aspies have very little choice about the conversations that we get to overhear, for example instead of getting to listen to what that cute shy brunette is saying to her friend, we have to listen to the annoying Valley Girls two tables over. These girls must have thought that the world revolves around them therefore, saw absolutely nothing

6

wrong with being so loud that other people can't have their own conversations or even hear themselves think.

It wasn't even as if they were discussing anything interesting. It was mostly useless jabber about who was dating whom. I mean seriously if they were going to be that loud they should least have had a conversation with some kind of merit. These kinds of conversations are rarely useful as learning tools about what to do, only what not to do, as who wants to be with, or like, those annoying people. To add insult to injury, they rarely let us film their conversations or take notes, and I'm seen as the rude one for simply interrupting their conversations to get them to repeat what they just said or asking follow up questions. For example, if one of the two girls in the conversation mentions a third girl named Sally and talks about how "she is such a slut," which is super rude, you can't be like, So tell me more about Sally, why do you think she is such a slut, what does she look like, and do you have her phone number handy? In addition, sometimes these random strangers that an Aspie might want to learn from don't even follow social etiquette. Therefore, we cannot apply what we just saw other people do to new situations.

For example, when we see a guy and girl sitting together and the guy interrupts his date, we want to rush over there and help him by pointing out that girls hate it when they get interrupted. Amazingly, however, instead of a lecture he is rewarded for it with a cute smile. Yet, I am 99.9% sure if an Aspie interrupted a girl who is talking it is not going to go well for us. In addition, we can't follow these characters around and see what happens after or before the conversation. This can truly be disappointing because sometimes one can grow quite attached to some characters and want to know what happens next in their lives. Will Kyle get back together with Nicole? Will he find someone else just as good to date or will his crippling debt be the ruin of him? Unfortunately, society has clear rules against this kind of thing. They call it stalking and it is frowned upon. In addition, eventually the subject will notice that they are being watched and this can change their behavior, even becoming hostile or confrontational.

This leaves learning in more indirect ways such as learning about people's social interactions through reading books and watching television. The problem with books is that they require you to use your imagination to try to picture what it is going on, since there are no visuals, and no matter how well an author describes the situation it still requires the reader to fill in the blanks and draw from their past experience. This is pretty useless, since social interactions rarely if ever go the way that Aspies imagined them. Our imagination, generally, alternates between two situations, one based on a heightened insecurity from past experiences of feeling that people don't want to talk to us, and that when they do, that they are secretly making fun of us. The other scenario, more whimsical and less grounded in reality, is that when we are alone we, or at least I, sometimes believe that l people will finally realize how great we really are. When we are out in public, our minds usually run through the second scenario, and we are constantly stunned when a social interaction doesn't go the way that it did in our heads. The side benefit of this is that we get to live every day with constant surprise. For example, is the next thing we say to a person in a social situation going to land us in more hot water or will we be rewarded with a smile? It pretty much makes going to the casino redundant, because, we feel like we are playing Russian roulette in every social interaction, but with crushing isolation and putdowns instead of bullets. For the life of me, I cannot say which is worse.

There are advice books that try to coach you through challenging social situations. One book I read was Neil Gross' The Game, and the Rules of the Game, which tries to coach you on how to seduce women. It is amazing how some people turn sex and romance into a competition with the other gender, thinking they can find happiness by being manipulative. Really, when you turn the other gender into some kind of marker for how successful (manipulative) you are, is it any surprise relationships between people are as messed up as they are? People with Aspergers are often the unsuspecting victims of all of this. When you have trouble reading body language, as we do, you have no clue that when you try to make friends with someone they will see you as another sexual predator intent on seducing them. Therefore, some people can be quite hostile to us, when we have done nothing wrong. In addition, we have no clue that someone is trying to take advantage of us. Instead of being on the lookout for manipulative behavior we give people the benefit of the doubt. If only more people could be more like us and treat each other with more respect. Alas this is wishful thinking.

Some of the advice in these books is things like when you are flirting, you should tease the girl with backhanded compliments, this will make her realize that she is not perfect and give you a chance. To an Aspie who is looking for a way of trying to befriend someone this may seem like good advice. When I was travelling in Europe on an organized trip with Contiki Tours, I tried to give backhanded compliments a try and told a girl, in Rome, after she made a really smart comment, that she was smarter than she looked. Instead of her feeling the need to prove herself to me and initiate the journey of her seduction, she just got really, really pissed and walked away. This proved to me that some books are really a horrible place to get advice when it comes to social interactions, and made me definitely wary of both giving and receiving advice from books. I prefer to watch how people interact with each other, how they tease each other when they are friends and how they flirt when they are interested sexually, what questions are inappropriate and are not asked, as well as other important concepts such as body space. I never know where to stand when having a casual conversation, having to shout to someone from across the room is probably not close enough, while, having a conversation with your nose two inches away from their nose is probably too close. Outside of that the rules elude me.

Therefore, the most useful learning device is television. Television is not perfect, as it generally doesn't show the mundane goings on. I mean, you never see characters going grocery shopping and trying to decide whether they should buy the no-name brand because its twenty-cents cheaper or the brand that they are familiar with, and like. There is never a scene of someone asking the store cashier where they can find deodorant or antiperspirants, and how they thought it used to be a different aisle in the past, and ask questions about when it changed. They only show situations that move the story they are telling forward, and events that are ripe with tension, emotions and reactions. Yet, it is often the mundane situations that teach us the most about how to interact and it would be the most useful to show them on television, since these are the situations that we most often face in our day-to-day social interactions. Despite that, television is still better than nothing when it comes to learning about social interactions. I mean, watching two people in bed is fine, but I am more interested in how he got her into the bed in the first place.

Another problem is that television feels no obligation to show events in real time. The characters can be seen arguing in the grocery store and a minute later, the program may cut to them making out in a bed, and you are left scratching your head as to what has happened in the meantime, for things to have progressed as they did. It leaves lots of questions in the viewer's head, like I thought those two hated each other. Did they phone home and let everyone else know that they weren't going to be home for supper? Or does anyone even care? It has got to hurt that no one cares about their disappearance for several hours without any contact, when they just said that they were going to be gone to the grocery store.

Television, despite the fact that the rules of life don't always apply, still has multiple advantages over other learning devices like watching a play or an improv show. For example, if there is a really tricky scene in a television show, which has been previously taped, if we don't understand what happened and how the two people ended up in bed together, we can rewind the scene and rewatch it as many times as we want. There is also the option of pausing the program in order to give ourselves time to think about what is going on and which social rules are being put in action that we can learn from. Even then, there is no guarantee that we will understand. Hence, our lack of love lives despite watching hundreds of romantic comedies and romance scenes. But at least taped programs give us this option of reviewing the scenes over and over.

Once we have seen what the actors have done, though, applying the same method in our own lives is a whole other kettle of fish. When the protagonist pursues a girl who is not interested in things like playing music outside of her window in the middle of the night, she suddenly changes her mind and realizes that she is in love with him. Even though I have not tried playing music outside of a girl's window, I don't think it would work favorably for me as I would probably be accused of stalking. Also I only know two chords on my guitar. Additionally, it's really a terrible way to send a message. If someone decides that they don't want to be with you the right thing is to let them go. If women really just want to be chased and pursued, which I have been told they don't, how manipulative is that? Aspies are much better at letting you know where you stand in the relationship, instead of messing with your feelings for their own sick pleasure.

One problem with watching television at home, however, is that there are often too many interruptions. For example, just last week I was watching a show and trying to analyze it, and my mom interrupted my line of thought to ask whether I wanted to come upstairs and join her and her friends. Another time I was trying to watch my show and learn about the rules of social interaction when a friend called to talk. I felt kind of bad cutting him short, but I really didn't want to interrupt my lessons. I mean, if it was really important then he would have got to the point instead of wasting time making small talk, and it really wasn't, really, that big of a deal, since I did plan on calling him back after the show was over. I mean, I have rarely, if ever, cancelled plans to go out and do an activity such as go to a music show or go to a hockey game in order to watch television, so it's not like I am that much of a loner.

I also hate watching television with a friend because there is something inherently unsocial about watching television and I may as well be doing it at my place. If I am with a friend I would much rather be doing something like tossing around a Frisbee or just talking. I also hate watching television with friends because most of my friends understand if I constantly want to pause the tape, or take notes, or tell them that they can't talk till the next commercial break, because I don't want to be distracted. Nor is television the be-all end-all when it comes to learning tools.

Really, there is only one way of learning about social interactions and that's experience. Much of that experience can be negative where we have to deal with adversity and obstacles. Obstacles that we can overcome and are as a result all the better for. As they say you can't create a diamond without an extraordinary amount of pressure and you can't achieve greatness without adversity and obstacles to overcome.

3. Elementary School Blues

I was never the most popular kid in elementary school. Who really does have mostly positive memories of the early years though? Not this guy. Those years are rough if you are different in any way. Having Aspergers is no exception. Sometimes, it feels like having Aspergers pretty much means having awkwardness down to a science, and what can I say? People can be cruel, especially Neurotypicals. I grew up in the middle-class, privileged, pretty homogenized community of River Heights. During my years from Grade Two to Grade Four, there was only one person who wasn't Caucasian in any of my classes.

Human cruelty isn't random. In mainstream society it has evolved to serve multiple purposes. First, it lets you know where you stand in the pecking order. Neurotypicals love their pecking order, whether it's tallest to shortest, oldest to youngest or even "coolest" to least "cool." I will call the coolest people in my class, Two Face and Tiffany. While I was definitely not "cool," I was a few rungs higher than the kid who pulled down his pants and peed in a puddle during recess in grade five. Plus, I was "friends" with one of the "cool" kids, namely, the aforementioned Two Face.

For example, when I was one of the few kids not invited to one guy's birthday sleepover (along with the flasher and the new kid who was a military brat), Two Face bugged the other guy until

13

he had no choice but to invite me to the birthday party. Oh yes, and have I mentioned how Two Face had made himself the reputation of being hilarious by humiliating me at school? I guess you need to take the good with the bad. I had a hard time reading social situations and realizing what was going on and that he wasn't really a friend.

I knew on some level that the way he behaved was not how friends were supposed to act towards each other, but like most people – even "not cool" Neurotypicals - I was so desperate for a friend that I figured that a shitty friend was better than no friend at all. Also, just as in any abusive relationship, while he could be horrible to me, he did make sure I was invited to that party … even if now I realize it was more to assert his dominance over the guy throwing the party than any real feeling of camaraderie for me. Also, he did sometimes pay for my movie. I do recall having some good times together with him. There was this one time we stayed up until two or three in the morning playing video games and then slept in a pillow fort. I realize I am not alone in finding myself in an abusive friendship. In one extreme case in Maryland, an autistic teen's so-called "friends" tried to run him down with their car, held a knife to his throat and coaxed him into an icy lake, taping the whole thing for their amusement. So I guess compared to that treatment, I had it easy.

It seemed as if no guys in my class had the courage to simply make friends with whoever they wanted, regardless of what other people thought. This situation was especially true for me, since I was obsessed with fitting in and thought that the only way to do that was to conform, and follow the playground societal rules. Unsurprisingly, I did not have enough of an independent streak to buck the system and seek my happiness elsewhere. If this were a movie, it would probably be about how I was able to overcome the social hierarchy and end its tyrannical reign. Everyone would realize that the people who had been bullied had a lot to offer. The sun would shine a little brighter and grass would be a little greener. Anticlimactically, however, neurotypical society won. It is still alive and healthy as ever, and we don't live in an Aspie Utopia.

14

Instead, I and many other Aspies have had to accept our position as a bullied outcast.

One of the biggest problems with being unable to read social situations, is that even if someone had reached out a hand in friendship, chances are I would not have been able to recognize the signs and realize what they were doing. Most of the time, people are too subtle, and their idea of reaching out a hand in friendship is giving someone a smile. What good is that? And anyway, how the heck am I supposed to know why you're smiling? Maybe your mom packed you an extra cookie in your lunch or has promised to take you out for pizza tonight. Maybe you just did really well on that spelling test last week. To assume it is because you are reaching out a hand in friendship is a pretty wide leap. If someone really wants to reach out a hand in friendship, they should just ask someone outright, to go to a movie with them, or invite them to come to their place.

In those days, there was very little education or support information about what the signs were that someone wants to be a friend and what a good friend might look like. That information is now taught as part of the Manitoba Health and Wellness curriculum. For example, it is now taught that a person should never put up with a friend who publicly humiliates them the way Two Face mistreated me. What a relief. Some people may think this is coddling children. In my view, coddle to your heart's content.

If this were an advice book – which it is not – I would tell children to stop worrying about things such as a pecking order, and encourage them to make friends with whoever they want to and can. But since this is not an advice book, and since I would be a hypocrite for giving advice I didn't follow myself, I am just going to acknowledge that the period of elementary school is an especially rough one for people with Aspergers. Another reason for bullying is that it forces a certain level of conformity on everyone. They think they know best. In their minds society would be in complete chaos and children would be running around buck naked, if they weren't around to bully everyone into

15

conformity. In their minds, it is the rare child who has the strength to not care about what everyone else thinks and really sticks with his or her perceived outlandish fashion decisions. Suspenders? Really? Now, suspenders are a great choice if you are dealing with a flood, or paired with cute yellow rain boots, or if you are working on the farm forking hay. Otherwise, people should not wear them, period. Aspie's on the other hand would say, wear whatever makes you feel happy. Also, back in my day, no one wore a fedora, but, I think that is mostly because no one had access to one or realized how cool they were at the time.

Wearing whatever you want and not worrying about other people's opinions takes the same kind of strength as it does to buck the social rules and the pecking order in which we all grew up. It could also have been the case that the few confident, strong children who could have changed things, were already at the top of the pecking order and felt that having the system in place was to their benefit. So I can fully understand the "why" part of the bullying equation – what confident, strong child at the top of the pecking order would change things even if they could? After all, it is a Neurotypical world that we live in, and all an Aspie can try to do is get by in it. I do, however, honestly believe that if Aspies were the majority, we would live in a more tolerant society.

I can kind of see the sick logic some people employ for why they bullied others in childhood, consciously or subconsciously, but what does not make sense to me is the way some of the bullying was carried out. For instance, I was usually one of the last people picked for team sports at recess, me and the girl with polio, and she was usually picked before me. This situation sucked, but okay. What didn't make sense to me is that when I got to be the captain, the strong players I picked would purposely not try. When I realized they were taking a dive, I changed tactics and would purposely pick players who were not the strongest just because I assumed they would try. You can imagine where this is going … yes, we always got crushed, and crushed badly. At some point, I began to suspect that even the worst players I picked were employing the same strategy, but since we were pretty weak to begin with, I could never figure out if it was lack of talent or effort.

This kind of behaviour seems like such a sick way to treat people, even for Neurotypicals. I mean, seriously, who does that? It's like cutting off your nose to spite your face. If their intended outcome was that my team would lose, guess what buddy, you just lost, too. Their hatred of me must have outweighed their love of fun. Bravo. Hats off to you. Not only did you deny yourself a chance to get rid of that excess energy from sitting in a tiny desk for four hours straight, you also took away from the fun of playing soccer, for yourselves and the resident Aspie who just wanted to have fun and fit in.

Another strange form of bullying some people do is hold couples parties. It's as if mainstream society evolved specifically to force people together, or face the social stigma of being single, a stigma that is ever-present in the Aspie's life. In high school, I was able to make some good friends. We would get together to play sports and sometimes just hang out after school and on the weekends. Halfway through the year, we started going in different directions. In a nutshell, they got girlfriends, and I didn't. I hate girlfriends, well, their girlfriends. After all, my friends and I have a shared history and tons in common, but as soon as a girlfriend comes into the picture, BOOM, the girl becomes numero uno. I wonder what they do behind closed doors to get that spot. I assume it has something to do with sex. I still don't know why they couldn't hang out with me and then just meet up with their significant other at the end of the night. I mean sex doesn't last more than twenty, twenty-five minutes tops. Let's be honest, in most cases, five minutes. If it lasted any longer, they would be marketing energy drinks for people during sex breaks. Any rigorous physical activity maintained that long is exhausting and would certainly require refuelling.

The worst time for me was when they started handing out invitations for couples' only parties. I mean, I'm fine if my friends hang out with other people or even go to parties that I'm not invited to … so long as I don't know about it. In my final year of

17

high school, one of the girls in Grade 11, let's call her Sally, got these really fancy cards made for Valentine's Day. She then proceeded to hand them to my friends right in front of me. She was then like "Sorry Adam, couples only. Tee hee hee." Boy, did I ever want to smack those cards out of her hand. I even went as far as seeing myself piling up those cards and tossing a match. I could see how, as those cards burned to ashes, the sprinkler system would be triggered, soaking everyone, while I made my epic exit, laughing maniacally, Sally crying as all of her hard work disappeared before her very eyes. Oh man, that would have been very badass.

What I did in actuality, instead, was absolutely nothing, which was, to be fair, super lame. At the very least, if my friends wouldn't boycott the party, I thought I could at least count on them to NOT talk about it right in front of me. But no can do. What's unclear to me is why they thought the party would be better without the dreaded single person. What kind of inappropriate things did they think I was going to do? Start belching the alphabet? Make jokes about how they were more fun when they were single? This is true by the way. Or worse, walk around in a giant baby diaper? Sadly, it seems that some people do not change as they grow older, gaining some new found maturity which would allow them to hang out with single people. The only real difference is that instead of their significant other being called their girlfriend, now they mix in some other words like fiancée or wife. Sorry Adam married people only, tee hee hee.

Children's society can be cruel, especially when you fit into mainstream society as well as a square peg in an oval hole. Society has developed cruelty like a natural antibody to tell who belongs and who should be shunned. We can't let an Aspergers get a foothold, because heaven forbid, if he did, we might live in a more tolerant, compassionate society. Therefore, society tries to keep everyone who is at all different down. As for me, I hadn't come to terms with my Aspergers enough at the time to stand up straight and say, "I am Adam Schwartz and I am awesome

4. The Academic system

People with Aspergers would have been more suited for university when it was a place of higher learning, rather than simply a necessary step to getting a job. We can spend hours debating something that we are interested in until we are blue in the face. However, universities like the University of Winnipeg, for the most part are no longer places to expand the mind, but are now places to get degrees to get a better paying job. This emphasis in society on extrinsic instead of intrinsic rewards does not bode well for people with Aspergers.

From a young age we learn quickly that we are different, and therefore get used to spending time by ourselves. We simply don't fit in very well because we think differently from everyone else. We may not get other people's jokes and they may not get ours. As a result, we get used to spending time by ourselves doing things that interest us. The more we feel like we have been shut out by the rest of the world, the more we create our own "little worlds," and lose touch with what other people consider reality; this is especially easy in Winnipeg, which s like a frozen wasteland where the cold keeps people inside for six-months of the year. And then, for another three months of the year this job falls to the mosquitos to keep people indoors.

Back when people went to university to grow intellectually there was a better chance that we would find other people who were extremely interested in what the class was learning. This would mean that we wouldn't go as far into our little worlds, or might come out of them more easily. When we feel we are part of the group, we care more about things such as how we look and how others perceive us, and try and fit in. That doesn't happen, however, with the way that the university system is designed now, with many Neurotypicals putting in as little effort as possible and not really caring about the subject matter. For a large part they are just not as obsessed, wait, no, that's not the right word, worked up, no that's not the right word, passionate, yes that's the right word, with what they are studying. Many people I met at University, sad to say, were not interested in finding out what Plato said; they were more concerned about what Jill said, and about why she and Kyle broke up. As far as many of them are concerned Plato can just go away as they are just interested in passing the classes and getting a degree, thank you very much.

In university, because of my problems with organization and the fact that typing up my homework or organizing my thoughts took me much longer than other people, I took only four courses instead of the full course-load of five. Having fewer courses meant that I was more able to fully engage with the material.

There is nothing worse than getting to a class ready to expand your mind, to find that you are the only one who read the required readings the night before, and therefore, no one else is ready to engage in a conversation that goes further than the text. This happened in my Introduction course to International Developmental Studies, among others. As a result, the professor had to pretty much just summarize the readings we were supposed to have done. This waste of class time was a pity as I had come to class ready to engage in conversations about the various issues that were covered in the text. There was a really interesting chapter debating whether the Marxist theory about how developed countries, such as Canada and the US, were keeping developing countries like Somalia and Nigeria impoverished, or whether another theory of development was more accurate. I had read articles supporting the different perspectives and was super excited to come to class to discuss them, only to find out most of my classmates hadn't been as moved by the topic as I was. Having the professor reiterate what the text said seemed like a massive waste of time.

Our professor had read thousands of books on the topic and had spent several years in developing countries helping with projects first hand, so obviously he had a wealth of knowledge to share with us that went further than what the book said. I expected people to be ready to ask follow-up questions about the material covered in the book. This topic touched very closely to my heart because I was born in South Africa, which because of the Apartheid system of the past has many elements of a first world country but also has elements of the third world. A doctor in South Africa was the first person to perform open heart surgery and its medical system is considered top notch.

South African distribution of wealth, however, leaves much to be desired. In one section of a city there will be these big wealthy mansions and a few miles away the poorest hovels you could ever see. This has led to the country to having a problem when it comes to safety and crime, because so many people feel like they have nothing to lose if they turn to crime when they see so much wealth around them. I figured that an International Development course would help me see how the problem was created and how South Africa has any hope of moving forward in lessening its problems.

Unfortunately, it seemed like my classmates were not concerned with South Africa, as they were concerned with what they were going to do on Friday night or who was going to be at the bar. Quite frankly, I had no interest in who was playing at what bar on Friday and would have much rather talked about Marx's theories of development. In my opinion, my cohorts' lack of interest in anything other than the bar and their social lives did not bode well for future generations. I was also extremely disappointed that people were content to do the bare minimum and show up to class unprepared. This made me feel socially isolated and like I had no one I could relate to.

One guy, Steven, who I used to go to high school with, at Joseph Wolinsky Collegiate, would brag about how he would start the assignments the night before they were due and still get an A. He wanted people to know how little effort he put into the assignments and how high his grade was. If he was motivated intrinsically, however, he wouldn't be taking classes in subjects that didn't really resonate with him and he would have started working on the assignments to learn as much about the topics as possible. Instead, he was focused on getting a degree, becoming a lawyer and in his own words "becoming filthy rich." To me this cheapens the point of an education, which should be to learn as much as possible so that in time you can make a lasting impact on the field that you have chosen and move the field forward or at least into a new direction. It also meant that the people who got the top marks and who I figured I would have the most in common with, and with whom I would really be able to discuss what we were learning about, weren't really any more interested in the topics than the students who barely passed.

There were a few times I thought that I had finally found people who I could relate to. Since I needed a science credit in order to graduate from the teaching program that I was in, I took an introduction to Biology class that was designed for arts students. Even though I knew I didn't have much of a future in Biology, as I struggled with science classes, I nevertheless buried my head in the books and studied hard. After all, I figured that even if I didn't excel at Biology and was unlikely to take it any further, it did not mean that it did not have interesting things to teach me about things such as osmosis. Therefore, in class I was always able to answer the questions the professor asked based on the material we were supposed to read. Had he been an Aspie, his questions would have required us to delve into the material further and would not have come straight out of the textbook, he would have required us to apply the knowledge we had gained. Since I was able to give the right answers in class, a few girls took an interest in me and complimented me on how well I seemed to know the material. At first I thought they were being patronizing,

22

because I knew I was pretty terrible at science. I thought they were just giving me a hard time for being an eager beaver.

Nevertheless, after a while I warmed up to them and thought they were being genuine, and even asked if they wanted to get together and study the material even though the exam was more than two months away. It really shouldn't have come as much of a surprise that they came up with a million and one excuses about how they were too busy to get together to study. The way these girls tried so hard to get out of studying with me, one would think that I had been asking them out or had anything in mind more than just getting together to discuss the course material. They frankly had no interest in putting any effort into learning the material than they had to. In every class, in an effort to make small talk, I would ask them if they had read the chapters, and they would say they had been too busy and then as soon as I left, would go back to talking about their social lives. As a result, I felt like I had nothing in common with many of the people I was in school with, and that I simply didn't fit in. It also seemed a huge pity that people wanted to simply do the courses to get by, and weren't allowing themselves to really get caught up in their studies.

Many people with Aspergers are well aware of our tendency to get obsessed, or passionate rather, about our interests. Other people can also get caught up in their interests as well, but it is rarely to the same degree. At times, the skills we gain from rabidly pursuing hobbies are marketable and result in profitable and/or satisfying careers. For example, consider Jon Elder Robison who wrote Look Me in the Eye about his experiences growing up on the Autism spectrum. He spent so much time with audio visual equipment that it led him to being an audio engineer and getting jobs with bands and ultimately landed him a job with the band KISS. He modified KISS guitarist Ace Freehley's guitars to do amazing things, like shoot fireworks when Ace hit a certain chord in a particular way. I am clearly not an audio engineer, so I cannot fathom how he did it. I can say, however, that it changed the concert experience forever and led the way for future amazing concert experiences where all the added extras are just as huge as the music itself.

I know that my friend and I went to the Black Eyed Peas concert not because they were our favourite band and had fantastic music but because they deliver a great show. At one point, one of the members of the band, Will.I.AM, came out through the floor of the stage playing his guitar while fireworks shot in the air. Robison would never have been able to reach this level of mastery, if, instead of focusing his time learning about things that really mattered to him he had been focused on getting the necessary credits to graduate with a university degree. This level of mastery requires time and dedication. As a result he was more ready to make a lasting contribution to society than most university graduates these days.

University would be amazing if more people were able to get wrapped up in their studies to the same extent. Maybe expecting people to actually take interest in their studies is asking for too much. It is possible that many people have always just done enough to get by. This, however, seems like a sad state of affairs because the desire to learn and to change the world has always struck me as a beautiful thing. Then maybe people with Aspergers would have a much easier time fitting in, and university wouldn't have to feel so socially isolating.

5. Rules to Live By

So the other day, I was just sitting at my desk in the downtown Winnipeg Public Library where I work as a Reference Assistant, when I noticed an attractive blonde and brunette sitting together studying for some kind of test. They were also chewing gum. Now these two could have been on the cover of the Sports Illustrated' Swimsuit edition. So, what did I do? As soon as I saw someone doing something I thought was breaking the rules, my immediate reaction, like clockwork, was to go over there and say something. So, I went up to them and as smoothly as I could, and said: "Gee, you guys really aren't allowed to eat in here. This is the Local History Room, and we keep all of our valuable books in here." What I expected them to do was to simply put away their gum and keep on studying. After all, I didn't see what the big deal was about in tossing out their gum. What happened was that they rolled their eyes and looked at me as if I had just said that girls couldn't wear jeans but had to wear long dresses and bonnets What they replied was, "Oh, Shelly, let's go study somewhere else." This response felt like overkill as all they really had to do was stop chewing gum. Nevertheless, I felt like kicking myself, but, what could I do? After all, rules are rules.

I am aware that other people would have ignored their gum chewing and simply have done nothing, because the library needs more patrons, and it is not for me to scare off the few patrons that we do have. Five minutes later, I was telling one of my supervisors that two girls had been studying in the Local History Room but had left when I told that they weren't allowed to chew gum. My supervisor replied that gum is not technically food and that I really shouldn't have said anything. Fantastic. Just Great. Not only did I scare off two more patrons, but I scared off two cute girls who would have been fun to gaze upon while time dragged along in slow motion, during my shift. I didn't need to embarrass myself and really shouldn't have said anything. To add insult to injury, I was being told by my supervisor that I was wrong for enforcing the rules. After all, the rules said no food and drinks, and if they wanted there to be any exceptions, it should have been clearly stated. In my head, it was quite simple: anything you put in your mouth is either food, drinks or medication. So the signs should have said, "No food or drinks, except gum." How was I supposed to know how to react to this situation? Some people would have used their own discretion, but if we are supposed to use our own discretion to make decisions about whether to enforce the rules, then what is the point of having rules in the first place? They shouldn't even be called rules, just suggestions.

I try to apply the rules pretty unilaterally and treat everyone in the same way. I mean, I could have treated those girls differently because they were attractive, but that would have been stupid. Why shouldn't rules apply equally to attractive people as they do for more homely people? What makes them better than anyone else? Other people have no problem treating them differently. I remember waiting in long lines at dance clubs on freezing cold evenings, for what seemed like hours, without my jacket, (because I and every other young person there wanted to save the piddly two dollars for the coat check) for our turn to go in. In hindsight this was even more moronic when you realize this was in Winnipeg, the home of frostbite. Then the bouncer would go through the line, letting girls he found attractive skip the line and go straight in through the VIP entrance. A guy with a cute group of girls was also allowed to skip the line. This is somewhat understandable, yet extremely unfair. Some members of neurotypical society have decided that females are the weaker sex and for that reason they shouldn't have to wait in the cold. However, apparently waiting in the cold is fine if you are male. In addition, a group of friends shouldn't be broken up so that some people can go inside while others have to wait. What is worse, however, is that the bouncer didn't see anything wrong with keeping other women, who did not fit his idea of what was attractive, because they were slightly larger or had more acne on their face, out in the cold. In contrast, people with Aspergers like to treat everyone the same, just to keep things simpler for ourselves. After all, it is much easier to remember one set of rules rather than a hundred. Nevertheless, this must have been quite jarring for those girls at the library because, being pretty they were used to being treated better and the rules that the "ordinary folk" follow, not apply to them.

Everything has rules. It's just that society doesn't always enforce these rules, and it gets super confusing and annoying when you start thinking that you are the only one following them. In addition the rules in society are constantly changing and evolving and rules that you started with may have It's hard to keep up. For example, in gym class in grade seven, we were taught a version of Ultimate Frisbee, where a person can take three steps with the Frisbee before they have to pass it. The next time I played Ultimate Frisbee in gym class, however, we were no longer allowed to take any steps with the Frisbee, but had to stop wherever we caught it and pass it right away. So, the gym teacher kept whistling the "play dead "" whenever I took any steps, after catching the Frisbee and turned it over to the other team. Since this example happened over a series of classes, sometimes it feels to me like the rules of society can change almost instantaneously. Therefore, as soon as I feel like I have a good grasp on the rules, which take me longer than other people to catch on to, the game has already changed, and something that was acceptable last time is no longer allowed. I prefer it when the rules are clear and I know exactly what I need to do and what the consequences are if I don't follow them. For example, if I don't brush my teeth, they get gross and no one wants to talk to me. If I don't take the garbage outside once a week, my apartment starts to smell terrible.

Unfortunately, sometimes the rules are not quite as clear as this. Usually the not so clear rules are about social interaction. Let's just be clear here: there are no rules when it comes to social situations that are actually written down; that would be too simple and sensible. Instead a person has to figure out what the rules are by themselves, based on observing others who are inconsistent at the best of times. That is one reason some people with Aspergers feel more comfortable with machines than they do with people. After all, when you are working with machines, the same rules always apply. You always know where you stand with them. You input the same information; you get the same answers, every single time. When you approach a social interaction that same way, you get a completely different result every single time, which is enough to drive someone completely bonkers. A little consistency is all I'm asking for. For example, if you stand a foot away from someone's nose at the bar, they will generally feel uncomfortable and take a step backwards. That is the rule; you need to respect someone's personal space or they will not want to keep talking to you. When I watch other people interact and a guy stands really close to a girl, I start to cringe and want to go and stop him from making the same mistake that I just made. However, for some reason, despite doing the exact same thing that I just did, it leads to the two of them making out. It's mind boggling. From an outsider's point of view, two people are approaching a situation the exact same way and getting completely different results. Now, there may be more to this situation than meets the eye such as the fact that they are boyfriend and girlfriend, or that the two people said different things in the social interaction, or that there is some kind of sign that one person picked up and that I didn't. The truth is I really don't care what people's thought processes are behind their actions. I am not a mind reader, nor can I figure out what their intentions are, based on the signals they are sending. Nor should I be expected to be one. So, if they deviate from the rules, no matter how good they think their reasoning is, it is completely confusing, frustrating and agitating.

The only way I can cope with or handle a social situation is by following the rules I know about, so that no matter what the other person is thinking or feeling, I at least know what to expect will happen next; it's just like inputting information into a computer. After all, rules are rational, while the feelings that guide Neurotypicals' behaviour are often irrational and impossible to read, and may change as quickly as the flow of the wind. To me interacting with people should be like algebraic equations that need to be solved; if A is true and B is true, then C has to be true, no matter how good the other person's reasoning. If instead of A + B = C in some situations, A + B = D or even   A + B = E in others, then I am completely and utterly lost. That calculation just seems wrong, and my brain just keeps repeating "system error" over and over again, to the point that it just freezes up. With this meltdown, anything can come out of my mouth I have very little control over the situation, but may have to pay a price for it later.

Ultimately, since the majority of people don't operate like I do, which I might add would make the world a more reasonable and less scary place, I end up in uncomfortable positions. For example, the other day I was out with some friends, when one of them, let's call her Alizza, decided to buy everyone else a drink, except for me. In her head, I am sure that this action was not personal, and that she had, what she thought, were very good reasons for doing what she did. I will never know exactly what she was thinking.

Here are some of the reasons that I have imagined to make sense of the situation. She only bought drinks for her best friends (which I wasn't), one last time before she went on the road; I am not a big drinker, and therefore she figured it would have been a waste of money; I might have said "no" so she simply skipped that step and ordered everyone else drinks; she just wanted me to leave her and her friends alone and regretted inviting me to her friend's concert in the first place(very unlikely since I am pretty awesome); she wasn't thinking anything at the time. All I know with certainty is what I thought, how I felt, which was hurt, and that her actions went against the rules in my head about the appropriate way to behave in this situation.

In kindergarten, we were taught that if you are going to share with a group of people, you should share with everyone, and not exclude one individual since that action is very hurtful. It is possible that her kindergarten teacher didn't teach her the same things, or that there was another more important rule that I didn't learn. Who knows? Maybe I missed a day. The teachers, aware that most things people learn in school ultimately don't stick with their students, probably thought that everyone would use their own judgement and that most people would adhere to the same flawed logic for reading the situation, failing to take into account Aspies. This is possible, because at the time I grew up, there weren't as many of us being diagnosed. Ultimately, there must have been some piece of information that I was missing. Nevertheless, she was breaking a rule, and the result was that someone's feelings were hurt, mine. And then, when I decided to call her on it so that she could apologize and realize that what she had done was wrong and that her actions looked cheap, she got extremely pissed off. Most people would not have made such a big deal of such a small incident, but the fact that such a big social rule was broken needed to be acknowledged in my mind. Let's be honest, if people don't follow rules, the result will be complete and utter chaos, shortly followed by a Mad Max-like dystopia. This following of rules can make me seem quite awkward to others. Other than people with Aspergers, the only people who follow rules as closely, are "bros" stupid "bros." I am so jealous because their rules have actually been written and passed down in a book they call the Bro Bible. This text has been referred to by famous "bros" like the character Barney Stinson from the television show How I Met Your Mother.

Some social rules I thought I had observed and understood, were location specific, but even that nuance turned out to be misleading. For example, in one conversation at the bar, another comedian's girlfriend had no problem touching my arm and my stomach as if I were the Buddha, and she was trying to rub it for good luck. I thought this behaviour was unusual, but I simply dismissed it as bar behaviour, considered acceptable for the bar. That same night when I tried touching the girl I was talking to, she looked at me like I was a ghoul trying to steal her soul through physical contact. It probably did not help my case that I wasn't a cute girl. To me, these were similar situations on the same night, so the same rules should apply. I did not try to figure out what was going on in either one of their minds. After all, that shouldn't have been as important as the social rules that governed the situation and should have given me a clue as to how they would react. I was unaware at the point where we stopped being humans and had to become an advanced race that could read each other's minds. But if that were actually the case, she would have realized there was nothing sinister in my actions and should not have acted shocked and offended. Therefore, it would have really been more beneficial for everyone if we had simply followed the social rules. Unfortunately, it seemed like the rules that governed these two social situations at the bar changed as soon as I thought I was getting an inkling of what they were.

In the end, I felt extremely confused and frustrated, because I could not get a good grasp on what was acceptable. Was touching someone else at the bar an acceptable way to get someone to really open up and feel comfortable, or wasn't it? How was I supposed to proceed? Especially, since there isn't just one set of rules; it depends on whether the other person finds you attractive, or whether you are male or female. Society would be so much easier to navigate through with a single set of rules applied equally to everyone, all of the time. Instead I have to deal with rules that mainstream society apply loosely, and are constantly adapting or changing, whenever I think I finally have got it all figured out.

6. Making friends

Having Aspergers, I have never been the "coolest guy." At
times, I have felt as if I really fit in, at other times I've felt, well,
like a square peg in a round hole. When I started attending Joseph
Wolinsky Collegiate in Winnipeg, from Grades 7 through 12, I
finally made a friend who was actually a good friend, unlike Two
Face in elementary school. His name was Moshe. His only flaw
was his obsession with baseball and wanting to talk about it every
chance he got. I mean, who cares who the youngest pitcher in the
major leagues was? Can we move on, please? We mostly played
sports, mainly basketball, when we got together, so we didn't have
to talk too much or deal with how socially awkward I was.

Over the course of time at Joseph Wolinsky, we also became
friends with other people till there was a little group of four of us,
Bethany, Moshe, David and me. Occasionally there were other
people on the periphery who joined or left the group, but the core
group, minus Bethany, have remained friends over the years.

Let me give you some background about the people in the
group. Moshe is my best friend. He has always been super mature
and the first one to tackle most challenges in life, such as like
getting a serious job or getting married. On the other hand, he has
even narrower interests than most people with Aspergers that I
know, and these intersts are all related to sports. Basketball in the
park? He's in. Watching Ruddy, the fictional story of the
undersized football player at Notre Dame? He's in. Going to a
music show to support David? No way, Jose Canseco (who, in

case you don't know, played major-league baseball for the Chicago White Sox).

While Bethany, was hugely into basketball like the rest of us, she never really wanted to come out with us to watch games. She would occasionally come over to watch the odd basketball game at my place, as I was the only one who had cable and got the games. But we generally saw her only at school. She was also a bit of a square peg, like the rest of us, because she was always dealing with serious depression, such as depression and weight which made her self-conscious. She is also the only one of the gang I no longer see.

Unlike the rest of us, David, is a brilliant musician, and his musical career usually has him on the road most weeks. In 2015, he even won a Juno for Country and Roots Music. He was also the only "cool one" in the group, and by grade 12, he was spending less time with us than when we were his only friends in grade 9 and 10. I knew it had taken me a really long to make this small group of friends and I knew too knew that we would all go in different directions, so I looked at leaving high school with some dread. I knew I would never be as close to them again as I was in that moment. Despite being a small town, Winnipeg, has the distinction of having two universities, the University of Manitoba and the University of Winnipeg. Most of my friends were going to the University of Manitoba. I was going to the University of Winnipeg. Still, I was sure I would still meet my old friends for lunch every couple of weeks, or spend a Friday night watching the Winnipeg Blue Bombers play, but our schedules would never line up the same way they did in high school. Heck, they had even less time for me as they were getting girlfriends, and their relationships would only eat away at their free time, even more than their busy schedules did. Quite frankly, I needed to make new friends.

A major problem arose that I could not have predicted: society has weird expectations when it comes to making friends. While I am always ready to meet new people and make new friends, other people I have met close themselves from making any more lifelong friends after high school. As a result, it is difficult to break into cliques. It's as if they think that they have made enough friends from high school. And, while I seemed like an awesome guy, they just don't have any room in their schedule to add another friend. Some of them probably think it's a shame, as we have more in common than the friends they made in high school, and if more of their friends had moved away, they might have had room for me on their roster. As it is, however, what can they really do? After all, they already have one tall, awkward, funny, friend, and that doofus is all they can really fit into their life at the moment. There are only so many evenings to go around, and if they spend time with one person, they no longer have that time available to spend with another person. So, they make vague statements like "Let's hangout sometime," but when I try to get them to set a time they are always "too busy."

On the other hand, I had always been told that my chance of finding someone I really connected with on a meaningful level would only expand as I was exposed to more people with a wide variety of backgrounds. People also told me that my uniqueness would be more appreciated at university. Perhaps I would even meet a girl and have a romantic relationship. It couldn't be worse than high school in this regard since none of the girls I was with at school with understood me or were willing to give me a chance. Television and movies had taught me that university was a time of hijinks, friendship and the occasional school assignment. So, I also looked forward to getting on with this next stage of my life.

I was super excited for my first day of university classes. While I had positive energy working for me, working against me was a lack of knowledge of social rules when it comes to making friends. After all, I had generally been with the same people my whole high school career, and so this familiarity meant that I had not had to worry about the etiquette of meeting new people and trying to turn them into friends. In addition, I was in the same English class as one of the people I was really friendly with in high school, so this situation helped a lot with my anxiety and fear that I wouldn't know anyone. I assumed that other people would be as excited about making new friends as I was.

The first day of university, I got to my English class bright and early, which was a huge deal for me because I am typically late for everything. I thought it would simply be a case of going up to someone in your class and being like, "Hi, I'm Adam Schwartz. Isn't it so awesome that we are both at the same university, and we both value education and higher learning? Let's be friends." I introduced myself to the girl behind me but she to pretty much just rolled her eyes and was like, "Is this guy for real? It is 9:30 on a Tuesday morning, and he is already hitting on me. All I want to do is settle down, get ready for the class, and possibly catch up with my friends from high school, and this guy is trying to talk to me. What a loser." She mumbled "Hi, I'm Brittany," probably thinking that if she just told me her name I would go away. Unfortunately for her, I had lots of persistence and very little skill at picking up the hints that she really was not interested in making friends, especially with weirdos who tried to talk to her out-of-the-blue on Tuesday mornings at 9:30 a.m. Even though she was probably wondering, "What's his problem?" I was wondering the exact same thing about her. I mean when someone awesome tries to be your friend, how closed minded do you have to be to not make any kind of effort to at least be civil? It's possible that I could have really understood her in a way her friends didn't because we might have really connected. We will never know, since she had no interest in making me her new friend.

I was a bit stunned at how poorly my plan was working, and how few friends I had made my first day. Fortunately, not everyone I met was as closed minded. I began to see some of the same people day after day, because we had some similar schedules, and they were okay with my hanging out with them. I knew one of them, Chelsea, through her friendship with my older brother. My brother, despite his flaw of being neurotypical, has introduced me to some great people who have a warm place in my heart.

One day I saw Chelsea sitting in the University Cafeteria so I asked if I could sit with her. She was in the process of sorting out her Human Geography notes and looked up and smiled at me.

She also invited me to come and sit with her. The next day, when I entered the cafeteria I looked for her to sit with. Bless her heart, she didn't get tired of me and kept letting me sit with her. Slowly, I got to her friends who all went to high school with her. Other than me, there were few people who hung out with them who they had only met in University.

I knew some of them from around, because they all lived in the same community that I had. I doubt, if I had talked to most of them for more than a few seconds ever.

Slowly, due to my persistence in trying to befriend them some of the members of the group she hung out with even invited me to come to their parties. They had great themes for their parties like a Lemon party where everything from the appetizer to the main course and dessert had to have lemon in them. It was a potluck/ contest to see who could make the most delicious and the most creative food item out of lemons.

I felt very fortunate to be included. After all, the group already had Ian who was taller, thinner and funnier than me, therefore, they could have easily rejected me because they already had someone filling that niche. In addition, while most of the members of their group definitely, didn't want to hang out one on one, there were a lot of people coming to the events they were going to, so they probably figured, "What's the harm in having one more person come?"

I eventually did become good friends with one of these people, Amy, and I still meet her for lunch once a month, since we both work downtown, I at the downtown public library, and she at her law firm.

Having Aspergers, I did not know why more people weren't receptive towards becoming friends with me. Was I putting out the wrong energy and coming on too strong, and scaring people away? Was the problem that I was accidentally invading their personal space and was unaware of it? Was I targeting the wrong group of people to be my new friends? The truth was that the problem had less to do with me and more to do with some people's closed mindedness. If there were other people other than

Amy and her friends who were interested in being my friend during that time, I definitely did not pick up on the signs.

It is true that there are many services available to help someone lacking knowledge in the area of social rules. For example, Asperger's Manitoba runs a social class which is fairly effective in building confidence, especially when you are in the community center where the classes are being held, surrounded by other people on the autism spectrum. Without the ability to read a social situation, however, there are still many struggles, and things like friendship or romantic relationships tend to move at a slower pace for us, than for people who are not on the spectrum.

It is also an issue of environment specific behaviour, and no social class can take place in a wide variety of locations, so the classroom material is not only theoretical. For example, telling people to shower regularly is pretty simplistic and obvious. But they can't follow you around and find out what your specific issues are, so they can't fix all of them. There are too many people with Aspergers with differing social skills, and it really would not be practical to cater to everyone on a one to one basis.

Also, it might have been useful to have more neurotypical volunteers, so we weren't only interacting with each other. For example, the French language learning program at the University of Winnipeg has French speakers as well as people starting to learn the language. After all, learning body language is simply learning another language.

Stand-up comedy brought the most welcoming group of people of any so far into my life. When I started doing stand-up comedy, sometimes I went to the comedy club and performed three or four times a week, just so I could spend time with the other comedians and the audience regulars. Once again, however, making friends and winning respect didn't come easily. One of the other comedians, who hosted a regular open mic room, even singled me out as being a weak comedian. Being seen as the weak comedian in a room of other comedians is never a great way to start, when it comes to making friendships. In addition, when I tried to further my relationship with one of the comedians, Ryan, by suggesting we get together to play Mega man on his Playstation were rebuked and it definitely wasn't because he didn't like Mega Man. A) Because Mega Man is awesome, and B) two weeks after first asking him he informed me that he and another comedian beat the game. Nevertheless, due to my persistence, the host who had previously cut my time short now gives me my five whole minutes, and has some affection for me in his heart, even if it is just a sliver. In addition, due to my persistence with Ryan, he and I are now good friends. I think if he ever buys a new Mega Man game, I will definitely get an invite to come and play it. I was also able to find some people, in the comedy community, such as Lisa who were willing to go for tea and crumpets with me.

Their companionship definitely sustained me during a stretch when I was really upset, because I was not being put in as many booked shows as I felt I deserved. It is my tendency to try and jump into something with both feet and then become disillusioned when I realize I am not as good as I first led myself to believe. It happened to me with hockey, basketball, acting, student politics, clowning, and almost with stand-up comedy. The members of the Winnipeg comedy scene made it easy to find people to talk to. They put me in their shows and sometimes, when they were being especially generous, even invited me to some large group events.

For someone who has always struggled with making friends, the Winnipeg comedy scene has definitely been fantastic. With the comedy scene giving me a place to be most nights of the week and the friends I made in high school and elsewhere along my journey, my social life has never been better than it is right now. While I am still the "uncool square peg," I feel I have finally found some people who are pretty square themselves.

7. Oh the places we'll not go

Another reason why it is hard to make friends when you have Aspergers, is that the activities many Neurotypical people get together to do with their friends are not particularly fun for people with Aspergers. Rock and Roll shows these days, don't cater to people with Aspergers; we are definitely not their core demographic. This has probably been the case since Rock and Roll took over from the traveling bards of old, and it's mainly because the music is too loud. I know I sound like everyone's parents, but I am afraid that this is the case. The problem is that the volume of the music usually sends people with Aspergers into sensory overload and it hurts our brains. It is like being screeched at for a really long time but having absolutely no clue what you did wrong to deserve this kind of treatment.

When I go to a rock show with my neurotypical friends in Winnipeg, they always want to go right up to the front to dance. These people do not mess around with their hearing since there is only a 50/50 chance of going deaf if you are in back of the room. There is a 100% chance of hearing loss if you are standing right next to the loudspeakers. I swear, sometimes I think I'm the only sensible person in the whole bar.

Therefore, I am left with two choices, to stay with my Neurotypical friends and possibly have the music drive me to the

39

point of insanity, or stay at the back and lose my friends. If I choose to stay in the back, my friends make absolutely no effort to accommodate my preferences, they just say, "Let's move closer" and do it without even looking around to see if I am with them. Then, if the venue is completely packed, I may lose sight of them for hours on end, and am all by myself for the remainder of the evening, which makes me wonder why I even took them up on the social arrangement, if it really wasn't that important for us to be together for the evening.

I even have to consider if they even really cared whether I came out with them or not in the first place, or if they just invited me out of pity. This is a bit sad. After all, I had some really hilarious commentary to make about the bands, as well as the other people at the show, if only they had stayed with me to hear it.

One would think that I would have learnt my lesson eventually, and started turning down the invitations I get to go to these shows, but when you don't get that many social invitations in the first place, you take what you can get.

Also, sometimes group members don't always play in harmony with one another, but they do their own thing. An example would be the local band, Mariachi Ghost, who amazingly are quite popular and well thought of in Winnipeg. A work friend at the library, Samantha, made me buy their CD, and when I finally got it and was listening to one of their songs, it sounded like every musician was out for themselves. I thought music was supposed to be a collaborative effort. As soon as I started listening to the band, my brain went into sensory overload and just started hurting. I was so overwhelmed that I had no clue what I was supposed to be paying attention to. Was my attention supposed to be on the saxophone, on the trombone, or on the drums? There were just so many different sounds coming at me at once, and they didn't seem to be playing from the same music sheet.

I am sure that there is some method to their madness; after all, they are quite popular. Nevertheless, listening to their CD was too much for me, and trying to take it all in. watching them

40

perform live where there are also visual cues to take in would have made my brain explode. Then there is the fact that most of their shows are absolutely packed, standing room only. If I did end up at one of their shows, I would probably end up in the corner with my hands on my ears and my knees up to my chest, rocking back and forth, unable to even think about finding my way out until the show ended, or they took a break for intermission, begging for the night to end.

This need to be in control seems a bit of a shame, since I imagine that the bands created their music to be enjoyed at live venues and I would love to go to one of their live shows if they took people with Aspergers at all into consideration. After all, the closer one is to the source of any kind of art, the better. For example, seeing the actual Mona Lisa is better than seeing a copy of the Mona Lisa and is far better than seeing a sketch of the copy of the Mona Lisa, no matter how good the reproduction is. When someone else repeats a joke he heard a comedian do, no matter how funny the joke was originally, the retelling is generally shit.

Another activity that happens at the bar, that is considered "normal" by Neurotypicals, but doesn't hold as much appeal to people with Aspergers like me, is trying to pick someone up. It pretty much always follows this script: it is the closing hour, and most people have gone home already, leaving just a few people in the bar. These folks are not celebrating after having had a great show or just hanging out with buddies. These ladies and gentlemen are on the prowl.

Is there anything more insane than the wee-hour bar pick-up ritual? Men and women eye each other, not because they are really attracted to each other. All the attractive people have gone home with someone earlier in the evening. The people left are scraping the bottom of the barrel. Sure, they may say that they are attracted to each other in the moment, but they know the next morning that they won't want to have anything to do with the other person. They would not even be eyeing each other if they did not have their beer goggles on. They know that they will feel regret the next day and be writing to advice columns with their problems. Not only will they have emotional problems, there will also be the large chance of picking up something, like an STD, since the people who engage in this last call behaviour are not exactly newcomers to this rodeo. So why do they do it?

If someone asked one of the Neurotypical guys why they do this, they would probably give you a funny look and say, " Uh, because it's fun." These guys only consider it fun, however, only if they are "successful"; those who strike out are not going to be leaving the bar with a smile on their faces. These Neurotypical guys – and it is usually guys – will pack into the remaining cars with their friends and be grumbling about the money they spent on drinks, and how it got them nowhere, assuming that for the price of a drink, the girl should be willing to "just give'er."

How cheap do they think these girls are? That for the price of a five dollar drink or two, a girl should be willing to have sex with them? How do I know about these guys? Well there are still some people like that in the group I perform comedy with; I used to be friends with a bunch of guys like this when I was in my early twenties. This lack of respect towards women is one of the things that I find the most frustrating aspect of this whole experience. Someone who is so willing to disrespect a whole group of people because of their gender, most likely also does not have respect for people with Aspergers; they are just out for themselves.

Equally frustrating, at least for me, is when women actually go for these guys. I always treat women with respect and when someone isn't willing to give me a chance, but goes for one of these guys instead, it makes me realize that, much as I would like to, I really don't understand Neurotypical women.

Rarely, do Aspies engage in this kind of bar pick-up behaviour, not for lack of trying or interest, (after all, we are excited about meeting people wherever we can and engaging in new experience,) but because this particular ritual requires too much talent for reading body language. We really have no clue where to start. Last time I bought a girl a drink at the bar, she said, "I hope you're not gonna try and kiss me," which was not only a surprise, but, made it instantly clear that she did not want me to kiss her.

It was extremely discouraging for multiple reasons. First, I found it discouraging and a little ridiculous that she thought that I was one of those guys who would feel entitled to a kiss for just buying her a drink. Second of all, ouch! By phrasing her response to my buying her a drink in such a way, it suggested to me that she thought I was repulsive and didn't want anything romantically to do with me. Therefore, I was getting rejected and made to feel inferior when I was just trying to be nice. In her defence, she probably had had experience with Neurotypical guys who didn't do anything for nothing. I clearly was not expecting such a strong negative response, so had no choice but to laugh it off, as if she was making a clever joke.

The guys and gals who do have this kind of "fun", risk going home with a few extra mementos like crabs or herpes, for the sake of one night's joy. Frankly, it doesn't even last the whole night and is more realistically 5minutes of joy, if you are lucky. Another outcome brings with it a reduction of mementos; if you are inviting a complete stranger over to your place, you may wake up and realize you have been robbed. There is also the possibility of being stranded in a new area, not exactly the best way of seeing a town. Then there are far worse possible outcomes, such as pregnancy, no matter the precautions taken. Yes, I have thought of everything that can possibly go wrong with one of these hook-ups, and guess what? No matter, how sensible I am, I am still sometimes jealous of these people. After all, who doesn't want to feel desired?

It always made me feel like there is something wrong with me, because I can't strike up a conversation with a girl at the bar, even though this is probably typical for someone with Asperger. It is also extremely alienating when your friends leave you to go chat up some ladies. It is kind of disrespectful of them to invite me along and then abandon me when they find someone else they prefer to talk to. Often, they don't come back to talk to me at all that whole evening. So then I spend half an hour just people watching, and go home. I could feel bad about their behaviour towards me, but I have had enough experience with Neurotypical society that I try to not let it bother me.

I just don't know how to initiate a conversation with a female at the bar, and I don't even bother most of the time, usually because I'm too afraid of rejection. The few times I did try to strike up a conversation, I came off as a blathering fool, and the girls raced away from me as fast as possible. Having Aspergers, I am not very good at making small talk at the best of times, and my questions just seem to come out wrong. Add the pressure that you put on yourself to look desirable, and you become anything but.

For example, at a Halloween Party, I kept going up to girls and asking them what their costume was, thinking it was a good opening line. They would answer the question, but I had no clue how to extend the conversation. One girl showed up as Poison Ivy from Batman. When I commented "You must be Poison Ivy," she replied, "Yep, I'm Poison Ivy," in a cordial voice, but when I tried to extend the conversation by asking her if she was Poison Ivy from the comic books or the movies, she just found someone else to talk to. I was left standing there with a million and one more questions unanswered. All I wanted was, what everyone else seems to get, which is the validation of their attractiveness and desirability.

Even though I haven't succeeded in having a one night stand or successfully talking to a girl in the bar, it doesn't mean that there aren't many other ways of having fun. Playing monopoly is fun. Playing the acoustic guitar in a band is fun. Snorkelling is fun. The only mementoes these fun activities will leave you with is happy memories. Other fun activities such as eating chocolate, white water rafting, and skydiving may leave you with more than just memories and holes in your wallet, but they are still significantly safer than sexual roulette. Heck, there are even fun things to do at a bar, such as watching a comedy show or hanging out with your buddies. Unfortunately, these activities at a bar didn't appeal much to the group of friends I was with when I was eighteen.

Don't get me wrong, I am not some kind of prude who has a problem with my friends having one night stands with people they meet at the bar. I just wish my friends wouldn't invite me along if they were going to abandon me halfway through the evening.

What I find really weird is that people prow at the bar looking for a one-night stand, and then judge an evening simply by whether or not they got any sexual action or not. Now those people are the ones who should be called creeps and creepettes. I am simply trying to strike up a conversation or trying to dance with a girl. Just because I am socially awkward and make one wrong move or say one wrong thing, it doesn't make me a creep. Life is painful enough without this hostility, thank you very much.

I would like to say that being a stand-up comedian has made these interactions at the bar flow more smoothly because of my new found confidence on stage and new people are more willing to talk to me off-stage. But this statement would be a lie.

While many Neurotypicals still mostly go to the bar to listen to music shows or try to pick people up, my life has become easier since I have made new Neurotypical friends who just want to go to the bar to do stand-up comedy together and possibly hang out, which I think is much more sensible. If one of these friends leaves the group to go and try their "luck" at picking up a girl, there are enough people that I am friends with at the shows, and I can talk to somebody else.

8. Jobs I couldn't do

One of my friends in high school, Moshe, was the first in our small group to get a job. His first job was in retail, and at the time, I thought, "Who really wants to work while having to deal with school and playing on the basketball team and everything else a high schooler has to deal with?" Granted, he was the guy who was the first to achieve all of the usual growing up milestones: the first one in our group to get a serious girlfriend, the first one to get a "real" job and, eventually, the first one to get married. The boring usual stuff, am I right? Don't get me wrong, I had a job during high school but only worked all of 7 hours a week as the skate patrol guy at the local community center. This job was definitely more than enough. Trying to balance school and playing on the high school basketball team presented more than a handful of challenges for me. Especially since I needed lots of time to unwind, and the usual schoolwork took me more time than it did for my classmates, because of my poor hand-eye coordination and the impossibly high standards I tried to hold myself to.

At that time, I was unaware of how hard it really is to get a job and how many applications you have to drop off to secure even one job interview. I had only dropped off one resume and had got the job. I hadn't even had an interview; getting a job seemed easy-peasy. I didn't put two and two together and realize that maybe the reason why it was so easy to get the job at the community center was because not many people finishing their final year of high school would want a job that had so few hours and paid minimum wage.

One summer, at the end of grade 12, however, when I wanted to get a real job which offered more hours so that I would be able to make some real money, I learned the old fashioned hard way that getting a job is extremely difficult; this is especially true if you haven't had that early work experience and you are on the autistic spectrum.

Do you know how many jobs or places of work are actively advertising for someone who is understood by their co-workers and customers only a quarter of the time?

In addition, the interview process to get a job is biased against people with Aspergers. If two people interview for a job and one of them has Aspergers and the other one is Neurotypical, there is a very high chance that the Neurotypical will get the job. People with Aspergers have a hard time making a great impression because of our inability to read body language. No matter how hard we work at it, we are never going to make as good a first impression as Neurotypicals. Our brains are wired differently so we will have a harder time being on the same wavelength as someone not on the spectrum.

The thing, though, is that if we got the job we might in fact be better at it than the Neurotypical who makes a great first impression, but could potentially be lazy or/and dishonest. People with Aspergers, on the other hand, work twice as hard as other employees because we are extremely grateful for the job. We are much more thankful someone was willing to take a chance on us. Even if, as new employees, we have more seniority are more qualified than, and work twice as hard as Neurotypicals, they are promoted much more quickly than we are.

Another thing to consider is that, while the ability to make a great first impression is important, there are many jobs where meeting new people makes up only a tiny portion of the job they do, such as someone working at an archive managing documents, or as part of a car mechanic team. In addition, there are more important assets to some jobs such as a heart surgeon than whether or not their co-workers or patients like them right away when they meet them. For example, I would rather have a doctor who is socially awkward but has spent thousands more hours studying, because he has an obsessive level of focus and has a less busy social calendar, than the next guy. I am of course, essentially describing any doctor with Aspergers. Nevertheless, it is the same interview process and the same weight placed on that first meeting regardless of the field.

It is also next to impossible to get that next 'job' without early work experience. I mean, who wants to hire a twenty-year-old with absolutely no previous work experience? Therefore, I set off on a quest to find a job where I not only fit in socially but was able to manage the work. It was a difficult task, not only because of my lack of previous work experience, but also because I was horribly ill-equipped for jobs willing to hire young people with no special training or education, such as retail or a restaurant, where there is a greater emphasis placed on making a great first impression.

I could never be in sales, no matter whether in fashion, or electronics, or any other goods, where I would have to approach people in order to have to try and sell some kind of product. Don't you just hate those really pushy sales people who pester you? Well, that is definitely not me. I use more of a hands off, wait until the customer asks a question, kind of approach. While I think this approach is much better, many people think you should be friendlier and go and introduce yourself. They are so used to store people pestering them that when someone just lets them browse at their own leisure they think the employees are stand-offish and not friendly.

I am also terrible at upselling to customers because I thought the point is to help them not add to the profit margin of some faceless corporation. That can mean that I often don't come off as a team player to middle-management who, when a person walks in, seeonly a bunch of dollar bills.

Note: If you are a middle-manager at a chain store, I'm not referring to you when I say that they are just out to make money, I mean the other guy, the guy not reading my book.

This is terrible for people with Aspergers as we are extremely straightforward and honest to a fault, and therefore, terrible at convincing someone to buy a more deluxe version of the product when the original product will more than meet their demands.

Why try to convince someone to buy an espresso machine that will also make lattes when the person will never make one. This usually means that I'm not the employee who would get Employee of the Month awards or even a good recommendation when applying for the next position. So be it. I would rather keep my integrity than win the free ham that they give the Employee of the Month in some places.

On the other hand, stores like family shops used to be all about making personal connections with the clientele, a place where you could develop relationships with the patrons, instead of people coming in only once, which makes that first impression that much more important. In the past, when people used to be loyal to their local stores, it was possible for someone with Aspergers to thrive in such an environment. As the neurotypical patrons and the Aspie employees had time to warm up to each other over the course of a longer period.

In those situations, people with Aspergers had all the tools to succeed, as we are hard-working, considerate and caring people. Now, it seems many people just want to get the lowest prices on their purchases, no matter what. Yes, lately there has been some pushback, and some people, the good Neurotypicals and Aspies, care that the companies they buy from act in a humane way, but the majority of Neurotypicals people just care about shopping where they get the lowest price.

Another problem is that people are rarely very clear when they go into a store. For example, some people go into bookstores and ask for the book with a blue cover. Really! If those are all the details you know about the book, then save everyone's time and don't bother coming in until you have a clear idea of what the book is or at least what genre you like!

Some Neurotypicals are better able to figure out what you are looking for, based on your body language. A "great sales person," the kind of person who could sell ice cubes to Inuits, the good honest guys and gals who make up the salesmanship Hall of Fame are able to read someone's body language and realize what they are really after and then sell them the much more expensive version.

Truthfully, most of us are not great, but only ordinary. People who work at stores shouldn't have to be mind readers. In addition, if you have something to say, use your words; that's what they're for; don't expect me, to figure out what you want based on your body language; this is not charades.

Feel free to browse around the store, but, don't bother coming up to me until you have some more information to go on than the fact it has a blue cover. If you want help finding any book with a blue cover, or are just looking for general suggestions, I am more than willing to chat. However, if you are looking for a specific book and think that a blue cover is enough of a clue to go on, let me inform you it really is not!

Finally, shopping should be about getting the customer what they want; therefore, there should be no need for a sales pitch or wooing, beyond helping to find the product and presenting the basic facts.

In the kind of environment I've described a person with Aspergers could work in retail and find some kind of enjoyment in it. Unfortunately, with the way it is currently set up, there is far too much emphasis on first impressions and financial bottom lines.

Another of my friend's first jobs was in a restaurant. It seemed the servers were always walking away at the end of the night with money in their pockets, because they always got good tips, really great deals on their meals, and prestige up the ying yang. I was a bit jealous, but I was also honest enough with myself to realize that I could never be a server.

I would have so much sensory overload as there is always so much going on at a busy restaurant. I mean, there are a million and one loud conversations, and people expect you to quickly record what they have ordered while three other people at the table are having a conversation. Sometimes it's so much that I want to ask everyone very politely if they could please shut up. These large groups who can't stop talking for two seconds are almost always Neurotypicals, because people with Aspergers generally don't like to go for meals in large groups. We find it distracting and at times overwhelming. In addition, we don't find it as difficult to prioritize the conversations and stop the conversation we are in, long enough to give our orders, like other people do.

Unfortunately, most Neurotypicals don't see it as unnecessary chatter, or that they are causing any kind of problems, because their behaviour didn't affect their last waiter's ability to take their orders. It makes me want to go "La di frickin da." I am not your last waiter, and if you don't cut it out, no one is getting served. People get really annoyed when you get them to repeat themselves for the third time.

I mean, what's the big deal? After all, it's their own fault they spoke too fast, not clearly enough, or too quietly the first time, or that their friends were too noisy. Once again, this situation is annoying for both sides. I don't want continually to be forced to go around telling people I have a disability, and they really don't see what the big problem is and why the waiter just can't get with the program.

Another annoying habit that many Neurotypicals have is to take a million and one photos. I mean, really, is it necessary to take a picture of your burger and put it on Twitter just so everyone knows what you ate? No person with Aspergers would ever do this because we are simply too practical. This is just how we are wired; we don't need to share everything. When we are done at the bar, we can just let everyone know we are leaving, or even just leave without saying goodbye. When I go anywhere with my neurotypical brother, he seems to need to have a conversation with each person on his way out.

51

Also, as a result of my poor hand-eye coordination and my struggles multitasking, I would imagine it would often take me a while to write down each order based on my struggles taking notes in high school and university. Therefore, because of my slower speed by the time I get back with people's orders they are annoyed that it took so long.

Some menus have numbers so you can just write down the number instead of writing out the whole order on your notepad, but it seems people are never satisfied with an item as it appears on the menu. They always feel the need to have it customized just for them, because they are so special. They also get so annoyed when you get their order of no pickles wrong and bring back a burger with extra pickles. Then you have to spend ten minutes listening to the many details of their pickle allergy and how you screwed up after you already apologized.

Then there is the fact that servers need to be extremely organized and remember not only what table ordered what but also who at what table ordered what. Yes, servers make mistakes, and they might have temporarily given me someone else's orders at the table, but it's still extremely impressive that it was at least the right table, and I would most likely be unable do that kind of job in the long term with enough accuracy.

Another aspect of being a being a server is the soft skill of being able to make small talk, but not becoming too comfortable with someone. I probably come off as very standoffish to people who don't know me very well, since I don't put out the right signs. As a result, people may prefer to be seated in another server's section, a server who creates a warmer, friendlier impression and can make small talk without crossing any boundaries. This expectation of the server is a bit ridiculous; servers are there to get your food, not to chat and hang out as many Neurotypicals seem to think.

One time, my brother and I went to this restaurant where he knew the waitress and she came over and sat with us when she was supposed to be getting other people their food. She even stole one of my French fries. More importantly, I was trying to have one-on-

one time with my brother, but when she joined us, all my brother's attention went to her and I felt completely ignored and cheated of my brother's attention by her. I would definitely not be that kind of server.

In addition, since my brain is wired differently, sometimes I say things that I think are appropriate, which no one else does, and would definitely not say to a stranger. I, on the other hand, don't think any topic is taboo and definitely would not beat around the bush when I have questions. For example, people don't appreciate it when you take their order and then ask if you can serve them better or whether they plan on breastfeeding their baby while they are there.

Retail and jobs in the food industry make up most of people's early job experiences. Since these jobs are not really appropriate for people with Aspergers and since there is such a high rate of unemployment in our community, I was lucky to be able to get my first job as the River Heights Community Center skate patrol, which I loved and held from the age of sixteen till I was nineteen. At nineteen, I was able to get a job at the public library with enough hours. My job at the community center was the ideal job for me in many ways. It was fairly slow-paced other than the ten minutes when the doors first opened to the public.

It was also a chance to sharpen up my skating skills since I had just started Senior Men's hockey after not having played the game in ages. So I would be competing against people who had been playing more regularly in recent years than I had been. In high school I had focused almost exclusively on basketball and only played the odd game of pickup hockey at the local community center two or three times a year.

But social problems eventually arose. Since most of my colleagues, who were much younger than I was, generally left as soon as they became sixteen, they didn't really take the time to understand me. As a result, they judged that there must be something wrong with me if I was working at the skate patrol with them, instead of a job where I could make more money.

One guy even had the gall to tell me there was absolutely no way he would be working as a skate patrol if he was my age. You know, because if I didn't share his emphasis on making lots of money I must have a screw loose in my head.

This conversation came about in a little overly dramatic scene at the Community Centre, where after getting one cold shoulder too many from two of my considerably younger colleagues before our shift started, where I pretty much followed them over to the canteen and practically fell to my knees and was like, 'Why are you being so cruel to me and denying me your friendship?"

Their leader, a beanpole of a male with big buck teeth, let's call him Trevor, even though his real name rhymed with Chris Bosh, told me, "Uh, because you're a weirdo for working here at your age, instead of having a higher paying job at a restaurant or in retail." At the time I was eighteen and he was fifteen and while this seems made up due to its dramatic nature, it really happened.

It might have been possible that if instead of trying so hard to be their friend I had simply accepted my role as that older guy who marched to his own drum, then at least I would have had their respect.

Who am I kidding? I don't really know what I could have done differently at the time nor do I know what I could have differently now, that would have somehow made them treat me with respect. No matter what I did, I would still have been seen as the guy who had broken the golden rule by not trying to get a higher paying job in retail or restaurant work and had accepted a community center job.

As they saw it, my turning my back on better paying jobs for a stress free job where I could just skate in circles all afternoon was akin to spitting on their Neurotypical values. As they saw it, I didn't conform and act like everyone else, so maybe it was a harsh, but according to their values a natural reaction to exclude this outsider.

Sure, there may be variations in how people act, but usually those are all variations within a certain range. Most people understand the same concepts and paradigms whether they choose to embrace, or reject, or ignore them. My behaviour, on the other hand, because of my Aspergers, suggested I was not even aware of these paradigms or rules, either in day to day interactions or in terms of values as such.

Plus, these guys all already knew one another, so they were more interconnected than in some other workplaces, and the pressures to conform and the penalties for not conforming were even greater.

I was extremely thankful for that community center job as it gave me the early work experience that would help me get through the door for when I applied for my next job. I finally found where I belonged when I started my next job at the Millennium Library, which is the enormous library in the heart of Winnipeg's downtown, working in circulation. I got along better with my colleagues because they came from more diverse backgrounds and the prior connections were not as strong. This situation meant that there was more room for variation in behaviour, and it was easier for me to fit in.

In addition, the work was something that I could manage to do, even if it was at times so slow and tedious that at times it felt like it could put you to sleep. I really enjoyed working with books and talking to patrons about them in a low stress environment. Even though one time an older female patron said that the women in Jane Austin's Pride & Prejudice were stronger, more independent women than Steig Larsson's Lisbeth Salander, which is ridiculous!

I was glad that I had been able to get that first job at the community center and I was equally glad when it was time to move on.

9. Sandwiches are beautiful

I am a simple man. I don't like drama, and I love sandwiches. BLTs, peanut butter and Jam, roast beef, whole grain, honey oat, and raisin bread. Sandwiches are so simple they don't require any cooking or very much work to prepare. All you need to do is put whatever you want between two pieces of bread. If you don't have two pieces of bread just throw your filling onto one slice of bread and voilá, an open faced sandwich. What I don't like is the sandwich technique that often happens in the workplace.

My supervisor, Scarlett, called me in for an evaluation. Let me start off by saying there is nothing good that ever comes from being called into the supervisor's office for an evaluation. My place of work is seniority based, therefore, the only way that you get a raise is by working a certain number of hours, and the only way you ever get a promotion is by applying for a higher position. It doesn't matter if you were the most efficient employee or the laziest one. As long as you put in your hours, you get paid accordingly.

In addition, they never call you in just to give you a private pizza party or tell you that you have the rest of the day off with pay as a reward for your hard work. Go figure. Therefore, being scheduled to go into the supervisor's office is sort of like entering a dragon's den, no, not like on the CBC show, where you get to meet with entrepreneurs; I mean rather the fire breathing village eating kind. The act of entering the supervisor's office is only done under severe duress, requiring prayers and sacrifices in the hope that you will exit again in one piece.

Now don't get the wrong idea, my supervisor is actually quite lovely person, it is my fear that a transgression I unknowingly made has finally caught up with me that scares me. People rarely tell you what you did in the moment; nope, they hold back that information for a special occasion.

Scarlett first gave me a form with numbers one to five circled to show how well she thought I was doing. Then she started talking. She laid out the positive, then she gave me the negative and then she gave me another positive. I came away from there more confused than when I went in. Why would Neurotypical society take something so wonderful like a sandwich and make it mean something completely different, something that leaves an awful taste in the mouth? Why couldn't they have named it after something I didn't like so much, like a tuna broccoli melt? Instead of feeling satisfied and full when I was done, all I felt was confused.

She had provided me with lots of information and feedback. Was I supposed to focus on the first thing she had said? Because by the time she had made her third point I had forgotten her first point. I was also not sure whether I was supposed to walk away from the evaluation feeling happy or not. After all, the evaluation sheet was negative, but she had given me two positive comments and only one negative comment and by simple mathematics that must mean that I was doing a bang-up job.

I have a hard enough time getting through my day without getting confused by all the messages that people give me. I mean, there is the tonal message, there is the information that they are trying to convey with their body, and the coincidental body language that they are unaware that they are sending. Once you add it all together that's a lot of information which sometimes can be quite contradictory. For example, one co-worker I used to work with used to go around the Community Center with a frown on his face, but, when people asked him how he was doing, he would say he was doing great, "Really frickin, fantastic." I really would expect someone who is doing "really frickin, fantastic" to smile more!

Another example is the person who says they are doing great and gives you a smile, but, their eyes give the message that they really don't want to be there having that conversation. If you are having a bad day, just do what someone with Aspergers would do, which is own up to your feelings and let the other person know that you are in fact not having a great day. Then figure out a way to make your life a little less miserable that very day, such as doing some exercise and blowing off some steam. At least going to the gym works for me. Another way you can make yourself a little less miserable is getting more sleep. If I had a quarter every time someone complained about being tired, I'd have a really high stack of quarters.

When it comes to giving feedback, and you really want me to focus on something, and get my head around it, then be straightforward and don't layer multiple messages on top of each other. If my supervisor had just called me in and said, "Adam work on taking neater, clearer notes when you are taking the phone messages," I would have walked out and known exactly where I stood, and what my supervisor wanted from me. I could even come up with a strategy for how I was going to do better at the areas where I lagged. Instead, I left confused, hungry and in need of a Tylenol because of the headache she just gave me. This is not a criticism of her, I suspect there are plenty of people who can hold various messages in their head at the same time, sometimes even with contradictory information. Good on them. I can't do this anymore than I can cut in a straight line or draw a perfectly symmetrical star.

Some people may think that providing their listener with one message, one thing to focus on, if in fact it is negative, is too blunt or rude. Yeah, it can be rude if every time the one message they decide to communicate to you is negative, but, it doesn't have to be that way. Some people only comment when someone has done something wrong, instead of giving praise too when it is due. No matter how many messages you layer your one negative message with, if it is rude or offensive, people will pick up on it.

The English language itself can be extremely ambiguous and leave a lot of room for misunderstandings. For example, the words sure, probably, possibly and even the king of all the wishy washy response words, maybe, can be extremely confusing, if you are judging or making decisions based solely on the language that is used. I mean if someone asked you if you wanted a million dollars and you responded "Sure!" it sounds like you are doing them a favour, in a way that should be reserved for the unpleasant tasks that we all need to do. For example, I can understand someone answering the question "Will you take out the garbage?" with "Sure." But wouldn't they say, "Of course, or definitely" or 'Yay," if they were offered a million dollars?

If I ask invite someone out, and they answer the question with "Possibly" or "Probably," what they really meant is, "Yes, I am in, if nothing better comes up and I don't choose to just waterboard myself instead." Therefore, I always feel the need to seek reassurance that they are going to do what I asked, compared to if they had just used language that would eliminate any ambiguity.

Here are some examples of clear, precise words. "Yes" or "Definitely." It doesn't even need to be positive. "No" and "Hell no" also do a pretty good job of sending a clear message. I wish more people would be more precise and make better word choices when it came to interactions between Neurotypicals and Aspies, since we experience the world in such different ways.

I know some people disagree and think, rather, that Aspies are too blunt or straightforward in saying what we are thinking, and wish we were more "diplomatic" in our language. Blunt is really just a negative way of saying up front. What's the alternative-not to tell people things that they don't want to hear and try to spare their feelings? I am not saying I haven't ever done this.

When I first started working at the library and was in the circulation department, checking out books, people would sometimes owe money. If it was under ten dollars, they were still able to check out the library items and I would avoid telling them that they owed money, because I didn't want to get into a confrontation.

There was no point ruining both our days, just because they owed a dollar. In previous incidents when I had told patrons that they owed a paltry 40 cents because of an overdue book they became hostile and wanted me to take their fines off and even got in my face and told me how useless I was at my job, when I refused.

Yet, in fact, their problem returning their books on time or renewing them had absolutely nothing to do with me. When they renewed their card every three years, however, they had to pay off the balance owing on their library card. Then they would get even more upset about the fact that someone hadn't told them about their fines earlier, since the total amount now was a shock. I probably figured that someone else on the staff with more experience dealing with nasty customers than I did should deal with this situation.

The truth is if I had said something earlier, when I first saw their file, I could have diffused the much more serious incident later. This is a truth that carries over into other situations as well. like , the patron, I wish people were less concerned about sparing feelings, but were more straight forward As it can lead to a nasty surprise when people let you know all the ways you have let them down at the year-end review.

10. The friend zone

While I usually find rules beneficial in guiding my life, one unspoken rule that Neurotypicals adhere to which really cramps my style is that a single male and a single female cannot just spend time together getting to know each other without the nature of their relationship changing. I am unable to read the signals that people send about whether or not someone is physically interested, interested just as a friend, or even means me harm. By the time I realize that the girl I am friends with is or was interested in having a romantic relationship, the possibility for that kind of relationship has already been taken off the table and I am safely tucked away in the friend zone. I move a lot slower than many other people, like at the speed of molasses.

In addition, since I never learnt how to read signals or how to put out the right signals myself, some people, (scratch that, most people,) have a hard time reading me, as well. For example, I one asked this girl, Karin, to a dinner theater show, since we had a mutual friend, the previously mentioned, Alizza, in it, and I wanted someone to go with.

We ended up not going to the show together, and I went with the boyfriend of one of the other actresses in the show. It turns out that I love dinner theater, and some of the songs were fabulous, like their rendition of "Time Warp" from The Rocky Horror Picture Show. In addition, the guy I went with turned out to be great company, and there wasn't the usual pressure that exists when you get together with someone for the first time. We

61

talked about sports, work, and even our families. There was no way things could have gone any better, except, well…maybe, if everything was the exact same but he was a gorgeous woman.

After the show, Alizza informed me that everyone else had understood my asking Karin to the show as asking her out on a date. So, I looked really cheap for not offering to pay for her ticket. The notion that I had to pay for both of our tickets is ridiculous because it wasn't a date. It was just Neurotypical baggage being placed on a simple invitation from me to get to know Karin better.

Feeling bad about the situation with Karin, since I had just found out that she was "interested in me in that way," I took her out for dinner. And to be honest, I heard that she put out: she had made out with one of the other comedians, who I am better looking and funnier than, so … I was confident that I could at least get a make-out session from her. While we both had a nice time on the actual date, there was this really weird pressure, since we both understood it to be a date. I had been trying to avoid this pressure and awkwardness when I asked her to go to the dinner theatre show with me. That way, conversation would have flowed more smoothly, and I wouldn't have become all tongue-tied and made an ass out of myself. Any Aspie would have understood this, but apparently Neurotypicals do not.

Nevertheless, we had a good enough time that we also went on a second date. Since I couldn't figure out what Karin was thinking, and I thought that she was a more conservative girl than the other comedian's story had led me to believe, I did not rush the relationship. Also, the closer to reality it became, the thought of trying to kiss a girl seemed a bit intimidating to me. Okay let's be honest, I didn't even really know where to start … How do you kiss someone without your noses or your foreheads bumping?

What if I was really such a terrible kisser she no longer wanted to spend time with me? How fast are you even supposed to go in for the kiss? And then, once she has agreed, do you both move your heads in slowly or do you rush together? Does one person keep their head still while only the person initiating the kiss moves their head?

Another concern of mine, was, that my attempt to kiss her might get rejected and that was more than my fragile ego could bear. I thought that, in time, the friendship we were building would blossom into a relationship since we had some really decent conversation. This, in spite of the fact that I still couldn't say whatever came to mind, as I was worried how it could be misinterpreted or how it would make me look. For every conversation we had, it felt like I had thought of three other topics, which I shot down immediately before giving them a chance. I have heard, though, from talking to many people, that dating is super awkward for everybody, and people's friends give some really terrible advice, like "just be you." Okay, let's think about that for a minute.

(a) No one is just themselves on a first date. Instead, they try to be a best version of themselves.

(b) This might work for someone who is extremely comfortable with who they are (and is a Warlock), and/or is confident that the other person will like the real them.

To have complete confidence in yourself, however, is rare even among Neurotypicals, (and is a sign that you are either a Warlock or insane). It is especially rare among people with Asperger.

Everyone has their insecurities, no matter how good-looking or charming they are. I asked one of the Neurotypical friends I made on the road with my Fringe Festival show, Aspergers: A Tale of a Social Misfit when I was in Saskatoon whether he was dating a girl that I had seen him with. This friend was studying to be an engineer and has a gym person's body. He said, "Yeah we are dating, but who knows what she sees in me." It was interesting to hear this perspective, and by interesting I mean scary, since if this buff dude who was obviously very clever, was insecure and had doubts about why a girl would go for him, then what chance would a stuttering, flabby-bodied mortal like me have? This guy probably went to the gym five times a week. I am having a good week if I go three times. One of my stand-up comedy jokes is about how my favourite machine at the gym is the water fountain. It's true! To think that a person can overcome these obstacles and show their best self after only knowing the other person for anything less than a month is insane, and something any person with Aspergers would understand.

The bigger problem for me is that dating, flirting, what have you, is the pinnacle of social interactions where people are trying to be the most connected. They copy each other's body postures, ways of speech, sometimes even the way the other person breathes, and when you are having trouble picking up each other's signals, it prevents this deep connection from happening. Despite being able to do well enough (mind you, not great) in most other social situations such as making friends or job interviews, I have had many struggles with dating and sexual/romantic situations. For me, the only way of overcoming this barrier is by first, developing such a strong relationship with another person first that I can tell what the other person is thinking, even if I don't pick up on the small cues. That way, we are able to help and support each other.

Despite all of the things that might have gone wrong on my two dates with Karin, however, I thought that I had handled all the challenges pretty well, and that she and I had got on fabulously. To use an analogy, it felt sort of like Simon and Garfunkel; there were still definite quirks that needed to be worked out, but it didn't mean we couldn't create great music together. I was more than a little surprised when I contacted Karin about hanging out with me again, and she informed me that there just was not enough of a romantic spark in the relationship to warrant a third get together. Neurotypicals are obsessed with romantic sparks.

What is it? A darn carnival? How can there be romantic sparks when neither of you are comfortable enough to be your true self? There might have been sparks six months down the road, but then again who knows? It's kind of ridiculous. It was like she wanted to say she was different than all the other

Neurotypicals for giving a guy with Aspergers a chance and then dumping him for not being Neurotypical after all, for being lousy at reading body language and taking longer to get on the same page as her.

I, on the other hand, would have been more comfortable to simply keep getting together for at least a year or two to get to know each other better. As far as I could tell, we both were having a good time, and I did not see any rush for the relationship to turn into either a steamy hot romance, or to end. Unfortunately, at the end of the day, it was not up to me whether we saw each other again or not. We both had to want this relationship to work in order for it to have any legs. One person wanting it simply wasn't enough. Nor was it possible for me to fight for the relationship like they do in movies or as many of my Neurotypical friends tell me to. It really wouldn't be the first time my friends set me up to fail.

Like when Moshe told a girl, Shirley, that I was super cheap and would go to fancy restaurants and just order chocolate milk. Not cool, man, not cool. What I am trying to say is my friends give really bad advice. No matter what Neurotypical society tells you about a girl simply wanting you to fight for her, if she decides it's over, it's over, and there is very little you can do about it.

Another problem I have encountered when I've wanted to take a friendship slowly and allow it to blossom into a beautiful romance on its own, is that people often see a relationship either as a friendship or a potential love interest, and if I want to take the friendship slowly, I'll get friend zoned. My female friend will see me as just a friend with the potential of anything more dying out. The concept of the friend zone is just as strange, menacing, and permanent as the phantom zone and makes just about as much sense to the scientists among us.

After all, aren't the people we date and marry supposed to be our best friends? Isn't friendship at the core of strong romantic relationships? Physical attraction to the other person is either there or it isn't, and it shouldn't matter how long people are friends before they explore that part of the relationship. They should be open to anything developing out of a really solid friendship. People need to simply stop being in a hurry to label and categorize relationships. Neurotypicals are simply shutting themselves down from something that could have been great.

As much as I hate friend zoning, though, it is a concept that is real in that it exists in people's minds. It is a bit like in Peter Pan, where fairies' existence is dependent on the belief of children, and every time a child says "I don't believe in fairies," a fairy dies. I don't believe in the friend zone. I don't believe in the friend zone. I don't believe in the friend zone … is the friend zone destroyed once and for all? No. Well, it was worth a try.

Friend zoning encourages a certain mentality, and that people need to jump headfirst into a relationship, which is simply something I am not equipped to do. No matter how good I look on paper compared to other guys (and I look damn good in comparison with many!) the fact that I can't read people and they can't read me makes this method of jumping headfirst simply a no go.

In an Aspergers social skills class, I learnt some really important advice. People with Aspergers often face rejection when they try to pursue physical or romantic or even platonic relationships the "ordinary way," since we have a hard time assessing where the other person is with their feelings. Therefore, we should pursue relationships in small baby steps. For example, if we buy someone a drink, will they return the favour and buy us a drink the next time? If they don't, then it means they are not interested in moving the relationship forward. If Neurotypicals followed this same advice instead of trying to go from 0 to 60 all the time, then there wouldn't be so many people in really terrible relationships!

The truth is that the concept of dating has certain costs compared to meeting someone organically. Dating means that you have to set aside time to get to know the other person, which makes it a gamble, since each person wants to get the most bang for their buck in getting to know each other, compared to letting the relationship develop organically.

For example, both people have to put aside some time to go on a date with someone they may or may not be interested in. This is time they will never get back if things don't go well. Now compare that to a relationship with someone who shares your hobbies and interests, so you spend time together at a music concert or a comedy show naturally, without any pre-planning. See how relaxed and easy that is? It alleviates a lot of the pressure and allows you both to move at your own pace. It can sometimes take years to develop a relationship this way, as people may start other relationships in the meantime, but eventually it will happen. Or it won't.

I am friends with many beautiful women who would simply ignore me at the bar or if I tried to talk to them online. By meeting them through comedy, I am able to develop a relationship and sometimes even feel comfortable enough around them to ask them to meet me for lunch. It isn't a date. It is simply hanging out with someone you really like and to whom you may feel sexually attracted. Plus, by becoming friends first, it keeps the hope of developing a romantic spark alive were we ever to cross that bridge. At least for me. And to be clear, in my humble opinion, that is much better than the alternative, which is simply being rejected out of hand.

I don't think this concept of meeting someone organically is just for people with Aspergers. I know that this is not an advice book, so I won't advise, but if it were and I did, I think that many other people would generally be happier if they pursued relationships in the same way, taking their time to get to know each other better, instead of simply asking a girl for her number, or asking her out on a date. This mainstream approach has led to many guys going home unhappy from the bar, because a girl didn't want to sleep with them or gave them a fake phone number.

Many nice guys, such as me, find girls are rude to them at the bar because the girl thinks she is being hit on; she has to worry about her physical safety and is forced into giving fake phone numbers instead of simply telling guys that she is not interested in dating them. If men and women got to know each other organically, however, it wouldn't be as scary for either of them, and they might find out that they really liked each other. It would also mean getting rid of the concept of the friend zone. That happy change is just one of many that could happen if we lived in an Aspie society instead of a Neurotypical one, proving yet once again, that Aspies are better than everyone else.

11. Too much emphasis on couples

Let's face it. As an Aspie male my dating prospects are not the greatest. There are many reasons for this. For instance, a male with Aspergers has a harder time jelling with a Neurotypical female. There is nothing wrong with either of us; we are simply different, apples and bananas, and therefore may have a harder time being on the same wavelength.

In addition, while guys go for women who are physically attractive, Neurotypical women don't place as high of an emphasis on looks. For example, any woman who was short and plump would have a much harder time attracting a boyfriend, than their male counterpart. In Neurotypical society, plumpness is often seen as a sign that someone is unhealthy, lazy or really does not take good care of their appearance. Yet, there are many plump, bald guys who attract beautiful women. Why is this? Quite simply, women care more about charisma than appearance! Now, let's define charisma. Charisma is the ability to engage in an interaction with a person so that they feel that you really understand them or are on the same wavelength, based on body language. To reiterate, this is something that people with Aspergers are horrible at.

Some people may think, well, why don't you just date a girl with Aspergers then? One girl, Summer, even tried to set me up with her "friend" on the basis that she thought we were both socially awkward, which, while it may true, not that I believe it is, is simply not enough in common to build a solid relationship on. I mean you wouldn't go up to a fat person and tell them they should

69

go out with your friend because they are both candidates for type 2 diabetes. Nor would you go up to a dumb person and tell them they should go out with your friend, because neither one of them is the sharpest tool in the shed, sort of more like a rake. Yet Summer probably would. She saw absolutely no problem with trying to set me up with her friend, just because we are both socially awkward. Doesn't she realize that no one likes people who are socially awkward, not even someone who's socially awkward themselves?

Unfortunately, being superficial is much more acceptable in Neurotypical society than being socially awkward. Summer really wasn't a "friend" to the girl she tried to set me up with, she is obviously a silly twit[1], and I feel sorry for the fool who married her[2]. I don't know what Summer even expected me to talk to her friend about on that first date, about how no one else understands us? In addition, there are a million different ways of being socially awkward, and not all socially awkward people work well together. In fact, I think most people I have met come across as pretty socially awkward in conversation, to me.

At the same time, it is hard to find a girlfriend in the Aspergers community. Most high functioning females on the spectrum are more socially adept and therefore, many will not use services such as Aspergers Manitoba or dating services designed for us. This means that they are a hidden minority and trying to find them in the general public is like locating a needle in a haystack. In addition, they may not even know that they are on the spectrum.

Then, there are the minority of females who do use Aspergers Manitoba. I mean minority both in terms of women with Aspergers as such, and in terms of those who come to the meetings. The ratio between men and women at AMI meetings is typically 30 to 1. This is a really tiny group of women, and there is

---

[1] Okay, okay, she isn't a fool or a twit and I don't really feel sorry for the fool who married her, she is just a product of a flawed society.
[2] Another disclaimer, he may not be a fool at all. For all I know he could be a scholar and a gentleman

70

no guarantee that I will connect with one of them. In fact, it is possible that the only thing that we will have in common is that we both have Aspergers and the condition does not define us. We may have completely different personality types, interests and histories to draw upon. For example, I am one of the most extroverted people with Aspergers that I know, and I spend a lot of time in bars, whether it's performing comedy, watching comedy or simply having drinks with other entertainers.

The chances of finding a female with Aspergers in the bar, however, are pretty slim, as many of us deal with sensory overload issues, social anxiety and many other issues, which mean that most of us are less likely to be in a bar in the first place. While it is never fair to generalize. this has been my experience in my 29 years, up to the present time. Therefore, we may not connect or necessarily want to date each other, and may realize it is better to be single than to be in an unhappy relationship.

My friends don't seem to understand this. One of the first things a person asks you after they have not seen you for a while is, So are you seeing anyone right now? If you answer this question honestly and say, Yeah, you know, I'm really not seeing anyone right now, you can see their reaction immediately turn sympathetic. I may be overly sensitive, but it feels like I might as well have just told them that I recently lost my job and am living in a cardboard box on the street. Someone who needs to be pitied, but you don't want to spend to much time with, in case it rubs off. When you tell them that you really are fine and you have never been happier, they look at you like you're deluded, like you just said you like picking leftovers out of the garbage for dinner.

It is more acceptable in Neurotypical society to be in an unhappy relationship, where two people cannot even stand each other than to be single, which as a person with Aspergers I cannot understand. One of my female friends was dating this guy who would make disparaging comments about her weight or her intellect whenever they were out in public together. When I asked her why she didn't just leave him, she told me to mind my own business and how in private he could be very loving and romantic.

71

I did not believe her and from what I could understand she would rather be in a horrible relationship than single, which to me is ridiculous. But each to their own.

My friends with Aspergers really don't see what the big deal is; whether someone is single or in a relationship, it really doesn't matter to them. Neurotypical people, on the other hand, tend to feel the need to reassure you that there is nothing wrong with you (I know!) and that you will one day find someone right for you. Well, this is a nice sentiment and I really appreciate their efforts at trying to help me feel better about my situation.

The big problem with this sentiment is that they are talking about something they know nothing about. For example, in high school when I was lonely and single, people told me that when I got to university I would meet a wide range of people and finally find a girl who was interested in me. The problem was that in university and afterwards I met a number of great people, but none of them were interested in me romantically, and I got my hopes up for nothing. I would have been better served if they had pointed out that romantic love is just one element in life and, yes, I might be jealous of other people's experiences and displays of physical intimacy, experiences that I may or may not ever get to experience myself.

At the same time I have been lucky to experience many other things other people have not. For example, I have been to Africa three times and Europe half a dozen times, while many other people have never left North America. I have also had a hit Fringe Festival play that I have been lucky enough to take to several other cities besides Winnipeg, such as Saskatoon and Toronto, and achieve success with, and have had a pretty decent amateur stand-up career up so far. Therefore, instead of focusing on what I don't have, I should focus on what I do have, an incredible relationship with my family who all love me to bits, being a great role model for my nephew in how to overcome adversity, having a good group of friends and a very warm supportive comedy community.

I can't really blame other people for thinking that I am missing out or that I will find a person in my own good time. After all, that's what society has taught them to believe. From a very early age, people are bombarded with the idea that a man needs a woman to be complete. Nowadays, it is acceptable to think that a man could be completed by another man, but everyone still needs to be in a romantic relationship with another person. There is also the idea that there is someone for everyone, and that if you work hard and live a good, decent life you will find the person you are meant to be with.

I was at my brother's house the other day and when my sister-in-law told my mom that she had just taken my nephew on a play date with someone who had a little girl, my mom's immediate reaction was to ask my three-month-old nephew, was she your girlfriend? First off, even if she was, my nephew wasn't going to respond. He doesn't even know how to talk yet. Second of all, he is three months old. He doesn't know what a girl is, never mind what a girlfriend is, so why are people bugging him about hanging out with another little baby, as just friends? Even though he didn't understand the teasing, he was no more exempt from the imposition of society's values and expectations on him than I am, one day he must find a significant other and settle down and get married.

This idea has also been pushed on people for a really long time and can even be found in the lessons of the Bible. Noah, when he built the ark, collected animals two by two, never any single animals. Never a pair of kangaroos and their super awesome single kangaroo buddy. In many children's tales the protagonist is alone, and is looking for their place in the world, but is rescued from this fate in the end by finding their mate and going off and living happily ever after with them.

The only story for children that pushed this boundary was The Paperbag Princess by Robert Munsch, and this story was only written in the last 15 years. In The Paperbag Princess, the princess realizes that her prince is a complete egotistical dolt who doesn't appreciate her, despite the fact that she just rescued him from a freaking fire-breathing dragon, and that she is better off on her own.

Some holidays are created exclusively for couples. Valentine's Day is a marketing gimmick to celebrate being in a couple. Everyone knows it's a marketing gimmick to make money on couples, and yet people still exchange presents and cards. (another way of excluding singles, notice a pattern?). Even Christmas, a holiday intended to celebrate family, health and your good fortune, gets in on the act of encouraging self-loathing among singles. For many couples, Christmas is a time to spend together with each other, as well as with their families. It is always so cheerful when you are the only single person at the table, surrounded by family, who are all in loving relationships and have eyes only for each other.

Couples who don't want to deal with crazy families and their rituals often go away somewhere and have their own little Christmas somewhere hot, hot, hot, like Mexico. People who hate beach holidays can go snuggle up with their loved one at a snow lodge after hitting the trails in matching attire. Eeww, I think I am going to be sick. Do you know how hard it is to cuddle up by yourself? I'll tell you right now it's not easy. In addition, don't even think about trying to snuggle up with a complete stranger and their loved one next to the fire. They won't appreciate it, and might even call the cops.

Then there is the ritual of kissing someone under the mistletoe, which is highly romantic. My only question is where did this even start? I mean where did the idea of kissing under the mistletoe come from? I don't remember the verse in the Bible where it says, And then the Virgin Mary made out with her husband Joseph because they happened to find themselves under the mistletoe, while baby Jesus looked on. If anything, the Christmas story should be a cautionary tale about why people should avoid relationships. As far as we know Joseph was the perfect mate for Mary in every single way and is excited to be the first person to reproduce with his wife, and lo and behold! God knocks her up first.

Why would any guy put himself through this? He has every right to be cynical from then on. Every time they reproduce he has to worry about whether the child is his or whether God has created another immaculate birth. Such healthy cynicism going forward is enough to tear up any healthy relationship over time. The only advantage is that people during this time did not live that long, therefore, suspicions and resentment may not have had a chance to reach the boiling point.

As if this story, which some consider to be literal truth, is not enough to make even the most trusting husband/boyfriend a little suspicious, out of nowhere comes the tradition of a man and woman standing under a mistletoe being obliged to kiss. While some Neurotypicals seem okay with this, my Aspie friends are smart enough to have some healthy cynicism and would not go along with the story of immaculate birth or their girlfriend kissing another guy under mistletoe.

To be fair, immaculate births can't be that great for women either. It places a strain on the relationship to always have to explain to their partner that they haven't been cheating and the child is in fact God's. The guy will constantly be looking at other men who even minutely resemble the child and thinking Ddid this guy knock her up rather than God? "Honey, why does God look so much like your childhood friend, Kyle?"

Look, there is a lot I am grateful for in being single. I can do whatever I want with my time without having to worry about anyone else. I sleep a heck of a lot. Sometimes I can sleep up to 12-hours straight and then still have a nap that afternoon. That is not because I have had a long couple of days and I'm exhausted. No, it's because I love the feeling of a warm blanket embracing me while resting my head on a soft pillow. Sometimes I do stand-up comedy three or four times in a single week. If I had a girlfriend I would have to consider her interests or what she wants to do, but since I don't, how I choose to spend my time is up to me. I never have to watch stupid reality television like The Bachelor, or Next Top Model, like some of my friends in relationships have had to, or hangout with super annoying people just because they happen to be her friends.

I am happy not having someone mad at me. Some Neurotypicals can get upset at you about the smallest of things like how you load the dishwasher. I think that there needs to be a better reason involved if you are actually going to get mad at someone. I also am glad that I don't have someone giving me a hard time about my place being a mess or wearing the same underwear two days in a row because I plan on going to change my underwear after the gym on the second day and don't want to get a second pair all sweaty that morning for nothing.

In addition, I can be scatterbrained at times. Therefore, I constantly am forgetting things such as dates and physical objects, and I can just imagine any girl just having a field day with that. "What do you mean, you made plans today? We're supposed to do whatever I want today; it's my birthday." "Whoops honey, I forgot." For some reason I think that just doesn't cut it. I still struggle with remembering my mother's birthday and it has happened once a year, ever since I was born. Trying to remember a girlfriend's or friend's birthday that I just found out about that year would be next to impossible.

It is also extremely exciting being single because you don't know who you'll meet, I mean, there could be another hilarious comedian at a party I might want to spend all evening talking with. I could also meet a girl who I willfall madly in love with and that would make it really awkward if I had a girlfriend. Whether the girl I fell madly in love with wants anything to do with me or not is really not that important, when it is all theoretical to begin with. But just for your information, theoretical girls go crazy for me; it's just the real ones I struggle with. All of that is in the realm of possibility as long as I'm single and most of it goes out of the window if and when I get into a relationship. The most significant thing, though, is that unlike some Neurotypicals I know, I don't feel the need for another person to complete me.

12. Divorce an Aspie's Friend

People with Aspergers are never a woman's first choice. We often come across as socially awkward and inappropriate. We may not pick up on cues as to when to change conversations, or when to end one. We have a hard time making eye contact, which is an extremely important quality in a potential mate. But from our point of view, neurotypical people often have their values messed up when it comes to dating. For example, males will often choose women based on physical qualities that make them look young, an innate pedophilic tendency. Additionally, they place too much emphasis on boobs, which are essentially just fat, and ass which I am not sure how anyone can objectify and sexualize. Gross! Often placing a higher value on personality traits than on physical traits, Aspies don't discriminate by age. What we find really sexy is a woman who is tolerant, warm, patient, compassionate and funny, which is, granted, much harder to find among Neurotypicals than a pretty face and a tiny waist.

Unlike Neurotypical males who can find females attractive purely on physical qualities, Neurotypical women judge mates differently. They are more likely to judge guys by the way they are dressed, whether they are well groomed or whether their clothes suggest they have money which in turn suggests that they would make a "good mate". No matter how much of a feminist they are, Neurotypical women in my experience have generally been taken in more by outer signs of success than by inner qualities. They generally want a guy who will make lots of money, and will overlook the guy who will treat them with kindness every day that they are together. Sad but true. Women with Aspergers are more likely to look for more important qualities such as whether someone treats them with respect. Though what do I know, I have been unable to connect romantically with any of the women with Aspergers I've met.

Women are also more likely to find a man doing certain activities such as fixing a car, showing off athletic prowess or doing a bunch of other sexy activities, like getting a really great tax return. These activities that make a man sexier to women are areas that I will never excel at because of my Aspergers. That doesn't mean that people with Aspergers don't have their own good qualities. We are extremely loyal, kind and caring. I am the first person to make sure that everyone engaging in an activity gets to participate if they want to. I would go through hell and back for my friends. We are also very close with our families and value them more because we know that they have got us through many difficult times.

These qualities generally, however, won't get us picked over a guy who is charismatic, good looking, or wealthy or a combination of these characteristics. Do not get me wrong. Neurotypical men also have their values messed up when it comes to the other gender, which I have already mentioned such as placing too high of value on butts and boobs.

Therefore, I was amazed when Alizza agreed to go out with me. It had only taken 28 years to find a woman who was willing to give me a chance. I just hoped that it wouldn't take another 28 years before I finally convinced a girl to kiss me. I met Alizza and her friend Karin at an open mic at a local bar. I hadn't had high hopes going into the show as it is generally not the best-run open mic in the city and I pretty much used it as a venue to test out jokes. That way, if the joke fell flat on its face I would not lose as much face, in terms of my reputation as a solid comedian.

I first noticed Karin after my set as they were only sitting two rows behind me. Three comedians later, it was Alizza's turn to perform. I am not one of those people who argue that women are not funny. I know that there are many funny women out there, like Jen Grant, Elivira Kurt, Chantal Marostica and Tina Fey. I have noticed, however, that some women stand-up comics, when they first start out feel the need to show that they can be just as vulgar as any of the men who perform. Therefore, while Alizza was kind of funny, her set had more vulgarity than I would have normally preferred.

Therefore, after my set, as a way of striking up a conversation with the two of them, I went back to congratulate Alizza on her set. As soon as I started talking, however, Alizza told me how much she really enjoyed my set and offered me a hug. The physical contact made me feel all warm and gooey inside. Aspies appreciate the small things. After talking with her and her friend awhile, I went home and Facebooked Alizza, to ask her to go to Rumor's Comedy Club, which is Winnipeg's premiere, and admittedly only, comedy club in the city. I figured that I had nothing to lose. After all, what was the worst thing that could happen? That she said no? Who cares, after all, she didn't mean anything to me at that point, she was just a pretty girl. I definitely did not think she was going to accept because I am very insecure when it comes to women. Therefore, it was a huge surprise to me when Alizza did accept. We had a pretty good night together, starting with me picking her up from her rehearsal for the musical theatre show that she was doing at the time. When we started talking and I found out her life story, I was amazed to find out that not only was she older than me, much older, but she had been previously divorced. It made me look at divorced women in a whole new way.

I realize that I am not most women's first choice, simply because they don't have their priorities straight. Therefore, I figured the best thing a woman can do to give me the best chance of success is to be previously married. See, if a woman marries her ideal mate who is charismatic and charming and finds out that he is also in fact, quite flawed, then she may look for other characteristics in a man. Especially if her ex's flaw is that he is a cheater or a narcissist as some Neurotypicals are. After all, not everything that glitters is gold. Substance over style. Neurotypical people have a million and one metaphors about looking past charisma and looks, because, quite frankly, they often don't.

Do not get me wrong, as I have been stressing, there are some good neurotypical men and women out there; they are just a tiny minority and are as hard to find as a needle in a haystack. A bad divorce also means that a woman may move more slowly before jumping into the next relationship, and may take her time with the next guy before she's ready to develop romantic feelings. This lines up nicely with the interests of people with Aspergers, because we don't always make the most favourable first impression. But I am pretty confident that, given enough time, we can find room in any woman's heart through our positive characteristics. Still, I had the same challenges reading her as with any woman.

Nevertheless, I thought that I had done enough to warrant a second date with Alizza and that we had as much of a real connection as I have ever had with another person. But that second date never happened. She told me that she didn't date other performers. But then she began seeing another guy, a younger comedian, and that was beginning to blossom into a romantic relationship. At the time I felt absolutely devastated. I also felt that Alizza had led me on, by letting me buy the tickets and think it was a date. She assured me it was a date and she had been genuinely interested, just not as interested as she was with the other guy, Kevin, who was probably rich, charismatic, or good looking.

I eventually recovered and became friends with her, even though nothing romantic or physical ever happened. I thought that we had a real connection. That led me to postulate that I had a lot to be excited about as I got older, and that I would have more success with divorced women than with women who had never been married and had traumatic experiences. I am not saying that all divorces are traumatic; I am saying that the more traumatic and horrible the ex-husband was, the better chance I have with these ladies. Also, that many neurotypical men are awful.

I don't think anyone can really cherish compassion in another person until they have known what it is like to be with someone who only thinks about themselves. In my opinion, this is the only way that many males with Aspergers stand a chance when it comes to dating. Therefore, it is not unusual for them to begin having relationships later in life. Having them when we're young adults is another societal landmark that we will miss completely. In fact that expectation is completely inappropriate when it comes to us.

This can be annoying as there are lots of messages suggesting one should be finding your soul mate while you are still quite young. After all, all of the Disney Princesses married at the height of their beauty and youth. Many movie characters marry their high school sweethearts or meet in university. In The Other Woman, Cameron Diaz says that by the early thirties, there are no longer any great eligible bachelors to date and dating goes downhill after that. Ironically, Cameron Diaz was in her early forties when she filmed that line, an age in Hollywood most women are considered repulsive, unless you are Judy Dench, Meryl Streep or Julianne Moore.What Diaz says is true, only if you define a great eligible bachelor as charismatic and dreamy and are unable to have the maturity to realize the number of great guys who are now in front of you.

In addition, some people, scratch that, most people, don't learn their lesson and will continue to go for the jerks just because they are charismatic, good looking and rich, or a combination of the three. There is no guarantee they will change. I know one girl who went out for several years with this guy who cheated on her, when she was out of town. She was heartbroken; nevertheless, the guy was such a charmer that even though he had had unprotected sex with another woman, and had possibly given her an STI when she got back into town, she eventually got back together with him. Their mutual friends, however, were not even loyal enough to tell her anything until she had already slept with the guy and he had already broken up with her. This guy being as self-centered as he was, after getting a second chance, then proceeded to waste his

81

money on a drug habit. Not only that, but he was also extremely selfish when it came to the bedroom, something no Aspie has ever been accused of, partly because none of us has ever made it that far.

I am not judging him or her as I don't know what was going on in their lives that made them go down the paths that they did. What I am saying, however, is that she had her values out of whack and if, instead of going for the charismatic guy, she had dated a guy with Aspergers, she would have been much better off, because we are more loyal to anyone who shows us kindness.

Guess what? She would still rather date another guy who was more like her ex, who had treated her so badly, than give a guy with Aspergers a chance. Because some people never change. No matter how many times they get burnt they will still be drawn to the hot flame. There really is no helping these people, which is just a sad fact of life. And she had many great qualities going for her other than her taste in men, since she was smart and funny and had a great laugh.

The fact that we have to wait until a girl gets her heart ripped out of her chest and stomped on before she will consider giving us a chance can be very hard on the ego of someone with Aspergers. I mean it is hard to stay positive, and do everything that you need to do to take care of yourself, to be able to take advantage of opportunities, if and when they present themselves to you later in life. It is very hard to see all of your friends in relationships or hooking up with sexy girls, and to continue smiling and believing that you too will one day find love.

It is very easy to try to compensate for these hurt feelings by turning to food and trying to eat away the pain. After all, these feelings are saying to you, "if no one is going to want to love you one way or another why prevent yourself from eating another chocolate, when food and your taste buds never chose your friend over you?" You never pursue chocolate actively, only to find out that there was information that you didn't pick up on because of your Aspergers, that led you on to believe you had a chance, only to reject you in the end because of your flaws. If you listen to this voice, however, you end up losing because you are not able to take advantage of romantic opportunities as they present themselves.

There is no reason why you can't have the same joy you see your friends having with someone they really connect with, if you're patient enough and let the divorce process and bitter breakups do the work for you. You can still have the romantic picnics in the park or hold hands with a girl in the movie theatre, you'll just do it at age 33 (or in Cameron Diaz's version in your early 40s) instead of 15, like other people around you will do. Do not get me wrong, I am not saying that this has to be the process for all men with Aspergers. I can only speak to my own experience which has been especially soul crushing. I still have not yet found the right girl.

I know one guy, Steven, Moshe's uncle, who doesn't have Aspergers, but who only settled down and got married in his forties. If he had given up on himself it is unlikely that he would ever have been able to stay positive and make this relationship work. He is now super happy with his new wife. Even though society said that Steven should have settled down earlier and married long ago, and that if it hadn't already happened by the time he was twenty-five he might as well resign himself to being a bachelor forever, his story had a happy outcome. He did not follow the norm when it came to relationships the way they're portrayed in romantic movies.

But there is no reason we need to believe that they represent the only kind of happy relationships possible, or that we need to follow their rules, or we won't find someone with the right values when it comes to romantic relationships. So, now I wait for Cameron Diaz.

13. First kisses and snowflakes

Is there anything more sexy or more magical than someone's first kiss? Yes, practically everything, in my opinion. Like chocolate fondues or fireworks to name just a few examples. I mean first kisses are awkward moments filled with self-doubt and feelings of inadequacy. Most people don't even really remember their first kiss outside of Spin the Bottle, as it just disappears in a drunken haze. Yet neurotypical people make such a big deal of kissing. People believe that first kisses have the power to lift curses, wake princesses or even make people fall in love with them. People say that they can tell a lot from their first kiss, such as whether or not they have a future together or not. Pursuing a relationship based on a great kiss is nonsense and the relationship will most likely have the same staying power as Target stores in Canada, which is to say, none at all.

There are far more important things in a relationship like shared backgrounds, common interests, as well as similar ambitions for life. Yet, neurotypical people believe in things like romantic sparks, that opposites attract, and instant chemistry. As far as I am concerned, these people may as well believe in the power of voodoo. The trick to a successful relationship is to move it slowly and in small steps, the way Aspies prefer to do. My stories below show that first kisses really are not as magical as people would like to believe.

My first kiss only came after Alizza and I had already decided that we had no kind of future together, and we were going to try the friend thing, if only to disabuse the notion that the relationship was built on nothing but physical animal-like attraction to each other. I mean she had definitely given me a lot to think about up till that point, as she was the woman who made me think that divorced women were the way to go.

We had been drinking pretty hard that night after a comedy show, and I had already had three beers and we were in our second venue. I had started thinking like a Neurotypical male, which is one reason people with Aspergers make it a rule not to drink too much. Therefore, I am going to frame things the way my newly Neurotypical brain would phrase it. We had been flirting back and forth all night and I thought it was pretty obvious that she wanted me. I mean, why else would a woman be nice to you other than the fact that she wants to play tag with your tongue?

Therefore, when she came back from the dance floor and took my arm and led me to the bar to buy her a drink I knew what that meant. It meant she wanted to sleep with me. After all, that's how it always goes in the movies. The guy buys the girl a drink and in return she makes out with him. It's like an unwritten rule and you already know how much I love rules. Therefore a make-out session was definitely worth the five bucks she was making me spend on her cocktail.

When the bartender was getting her drink she made it pretty obvious that she wanted me to kiss her by the way she looked at me all starry-eyed. I felt like a white knight finally giving her what she wanted. The whole night had been working towards this point after our brilliant comedy sets on stage earlier, okay, my brilliant set and her decent one. Nonetheless, it made perfect sense that two good looking funny people should be making out at the bar at that point in the night.

Despite my good looks I was only a pretty good kisser as it was my first kiss, but, it was obvious that I was a natural at it and that the sparks were flying and hitting other people in the bar in the eyes. She even said that it was obvious that we had chemistry. Even though we walked around with our hands all over each other, okay, just my hands, she was just so blown away by my attractiveness she had to fight to constrain herself. If she rubbed her hands on my body she would be lost forever.

Therefore, it was a bit of a surprise at the end of the night ending up in a cab by myself. In the morning, however, as soon as I started thinking like my Aspie self, I wrote her a Facebook message telling her that it could not happen again, as she was seeing someone else and I wasn't even sure we could be friends without being unfair to her boyfriend.

She being a Neurotypical might get extremely confused, because I knew how much she believed in "chemistry." This girl even believed in horoscopes and astrology and as much as I try to keep an open mind about most things, to me these things come as close to voodoo as it gets without practicing witchcraft. The belief that things like our personalities are predestined by the month we are born, does not compute with an Aspie's logical brain. It might hurt me to lose her as a friend for a while, but unlike many Neurotypicals, I am really bothered by unfaithfulness.

In my head I am always the one being cheated on when I imagine myself dating a Neurotypical woman. Therefore, I could not turn around and do the same thing to her boyfriend. She was probably feeling embarrassed and scorned, and pointed out that I was the one who kissed her. In her mind it is acceptable to expect, nay insist that, your male friend, who has written several jokes inspired by you, buy you a drink, without expecting anything in return.

If a comedian writes a joke about a person, they don't owe that person anything because their behaviour led to the funny observation. Also, she must not have realized how confusing her body language was for me, or figured out that I was drunk, and thinking like a Neurotypical. Therefore, she was clearly getting me to buy her a drink because she wanted me to kiss her. If she later wanted to deny it and play it off as if that was not her intention, I am a big enough person to go along with her version of events. I knew I was completely in the right, but was willing to take on the role of the Rogue or Scad in order for her to keep her dignity intact.

To be fair, though, that wasn't really my first kiss. My first kiss came from a hot girl in a bar in Barcelona dressed like a pirate, who for all I know, swore like a sailor and kissed more men than a drunken sailor on shore leave. I was in Europe with my sister on an organized bus trip called Contiki, which I mentioned before, which was like a high school field trip except with a jam packed itinerary and enough random hook-ups en route that would make the wildest party bus seem conservative; therefore it was a great time to explore Neurotypical-Aspie relations. While having my sister there for moral support and to explore the cities with during the day was great, she was not as useful when it came to insights about how to further these Neurotypical-Aspie relations.

Information about where I was going wrong when it came to understanding neurotypical females or how to alter my behaviour so I had more chances to exchange sweet kisses with them, would have been much appreciated. Alas, to the detriment of the neurotypical females I came across, I never did figure it out.

One girl on the trip from Canada was going on one last hurrah before settling down to get married to a nice Canadian boy who was not on the trip. Turns out she ended up being one of two girls who had sexy times with an Australian guy who was much older, and she and the guy decided to settle down together in Australia, with the Canadian boy all but forgotten. All this because in her mind, after one kiss with the Australian, she knew they were going to spend the rest of their lives together. Some Neurotypicals, pff.

Most hook-ups, though, did not lead to something serious that way. I mean, Contiki might as well have had as their motto, "Take a chance, join in our sexy times. only one in a hundred encounters ends with a STD. Small print, if you have Aspergers we apologize, but even though you may be the only person leaving without getting laid there are still other cool sights. Look, it's the statue of David."

Some Neurotypical people are way too much into casual sex, but that's just my opinion. In Barcelona, during a bar hopping night with the girl who I had thought was cute and that I might possibly form a connection with, I thought she was coming around to me five minutes into the evening, but then she started making out big time with the Spanish bouncer, proving one thing only, that I know nothing, absolutely nothing, when it comes to women or intimacy.

On the plus side, because we were such a large group, every bar gave us a complimentary shot and then it was on to the next bar. By the fifth bar I was feeling pretty fearless with all that liquid courage, and started dancing with all these sexy girls dressed like pirates, hoping for some elbow touching or something. When one of the girls, probably the hottest one in the party, whispered, "Do you mind if I kiss you?" I thought, finally the reaction I have been expecting the last 26 years! Now my luck can finally change. I mean, this is only natural. After all I am gorgeous, I wonder why it has taken so long. God, Neurotypicals are slow! So in a cavalier way which I hope did not come across as too excited or desperate, and more like girls were asking if they could kiss me all the time, I readily agreed.

The problem, though, was that at this point we were both so drunk that there was absolutely no tongues involved. After a few seconds, she pulled away and stuck on my chest a sticker that says you have been kissed by the Bride to Be. In a totally hot British accent she said "Thank you." That was all. She seemed to think she was done with me, while I thought there was going to be more conversation.

I looked around to see if any of the other hot British chicks wanted to kiss me as well, since I am a such a gracious person and not about to turn down other offers. After all, my luck had just changed! Why wouldn't all the rest of the girls want to get in on kissing me as well? Wasn't that how it worked? No one wanted to kiss you, until the first girl did and then the floodgates broke open with everyone wanting to kiss you after that, after the first attractive girl had given you her blessing and acknowledged your good looks and existence. Apparently not. They were all fine with me disappearing.

So I reluctantly joined the rest of my Contiki party, and apparently everyone was happy for me. They did not see my changed fortune as a big deal, and no one wanted to keep going in that bar, or go to another, but just wanted to call it a night, and get a taxi and go back to the campground we were staying at. While I was disappointed the night of my changing luck was over, I was not heartbroken. I mean, I figured girls would be just as interested in me the next day as they were that evening, and I had to rest and store up my strength to deal with all the oncoming waves of girls. Alas, the next morning, nothing came to fruition and the only memento from the night before was the sticker. I went back to being the guy who was absolutely hopeless with the ladies. Nothing had changed.

Proving in my mind without a doubt, and hopefully in yours too, that there really isn't anything that magical about first kisses after all.

14. A League of our own

We need Sports Leagues for people with Aspergers so that we can feel good about who we are. I know this sounds like a middle-class First World problem, I mean, who cares about whether or not we feel good about ourselves when we play sports. "Oh, little Adam can't keep up on the ice rink, so he wants to take his puck and start his own league, boo hoo." Ha ha, so funny!

I mean there is already a precedent; not only are there Special Olympics for people with mental disabilities, and Para Olympics for people with physical disabilities, but there are also separate games for Little People. On the radio, they were interviewing one of the athletes, who participated on the provincial level, and he was talking about how it was one of the best experiences of his life. For him it captured what sports should be all about, a chance to participate and get some exercise, while making some good friends. These are all things that people with Aspergers could benefit from.

There is no reason why there can't be a League or even a Sports Tournament for people with Aspergers, since we generally have worse hand-eye-coordination than most Neurotypical people.

In addition, Neurotypicals put far too much emphasis on "winning" in every area of their lives, whether it be academics, sports, or even their sex lives. Do not get me wrong; I am jealous of my brother who was a two-time all-star for his high school division, as well as being a key part of leading his team into a provincial championship game, but that kind of glory doesn't last very long. No one wants to hear about how good your high school sports career was and a few years after graduating from university he stopped playing in a senior men's basketball rec league and has become a real couch potato.

Winning only takes you so far, while the feelings of being able to compete, make friends and get some exercise are much more important. After all I am still good friends with David and Moshe eight years after playing on the same high school basketball team as them. In addition, there is often as much pressure on nine-year-olds to win, or to make the highest level team, as there is for grown-ups, which is pretty messed up.

A story in the news recently featured a father who pulled his nine-year-old son off the local boys' hockey team, because the son wasn't getting any playing time, and would just sit on the bench and cry, as the same players kept getting more and more ice time. This was devastating for the child. All he wanted to do was play hockey, and his coach wouldn't give him the opportunity. The coach probably thought that playing the players who gave the team the best chance of winning was more important than being more egalitarian with the ice time. This was crushing the boy. I feel sports at this age should be more about development and healthy living and getting to be with your friends. I think it is better to win or lose as a team, and to play everyone. Some teams and leagues are highly competitive and people think this justifies not playing some players. But in that case, if the player isn't good enough to compete, then don't put him on the team. Let him play in a less competitive league. This is just another example of Neurotypical people messing with people's heads, filling their heads with hubris and having them think that they can compete at the highest level, only to have them ride the bench all season.

When I was growing up, there were a number of levels that someone could play at. Since I didn't have good hand-eye coordination, I wasn't a very skilled hockey player, soccer player or basketball player. Therefore, in hockey, I always ended up at the

91

lowest level and working my butt off, and I still had a hard time being able to compete.

This meant that whenever there was a team penalty and the coach had to pick someone on the ice to serve it, he would always pick me, which felt like a form of bullying and isolation. It suggested to everyone that sending me off the ice to serve the penalty would have the least impact. Having the coach suggest with this decision, that I was worthless and not worthy of respect taught my Neurotypical teammates that they could treat me badly as well. This was extremely hard on my feelings and made me avoid playing hockey for many years. A more egalitarian approach to sending players off to serve the penalty by the coach would have been much easier on my self-esteem and confidence. It would also have made it easier for me to make friends with the other guys on my team.

It didn't help that I had trouble tying my skates tight enough by myself. Therefore, until I was fourteen, my parents came along into the dressing room to tie my skates. That year, my coach decreed that parents were no longer allowed in the dressing room, because parents talk and they might give the other team our strategy for losing the game. Neurotypicals are even competitive in defeat; I have to grudgingly admire that. Alternatively, it could have been the inappropriateness of women being in the dressing room while players were in various stages of changing their clothes.

After that, one player kindly agreed to help with my skates. Was he one of the good Neurotypicals? Well, after this time, whenever I saw him in public in subsequent years, which was fairly frequently, he would bring up these incidents in an attempt to silence me or just make me turn beet red with embarrassment. This tactic worked as well to bludgeon me into silence as a mallet or rubber chicken would have done.

It would have been extremely beneficial if there had been a League for people with Aspergers, or even a few tournaments a year, where not only would I have been seen as skilled and valued, I would also have been able to compete. A League of our own would enable people with Aspergers to have more self-esteem on the ice, which would carry over into other areas, like our social lives. I think of all the ways learning positive self esteem during games, at a young age, might have trickled into other aspects of my life. For example, more self-confidence would have helped when it came to making decisions. My perpetual indecisiveness manifests itself often in the way I have a hard time making decisions, big or small, in case I'm wrong. I take forever when it comes to ordering food at a restaurant, for example.

Another benefit of an Aspergers League would be that the team could model tolerance, and make sure that everyone was having a good time, because we know that there are more important things than winning. Do not get me wrong, winning is important, but it should never come at the cost of creating a good team environment, where everyone feels like they can contribute to the team's success in some small way, and everyone feels included. Winning isn't a sufficient enough reward if it means a few, more talented players hog the puck the whole time. People with Aspergers know how much it hurts to be excluded, and make sure to foster a feeling of inclusion. This is something that came in as a distant second on the Neurotypical teams that I have played on, far, far behind winning.

In one high school basketball team I played on, a guy I had played junior varsity basketball with previously, never once passed me the basketball, simply because I had dropped a few of his passes that were too hard and too fast for me to catch in junior high. When I tried to talk with him about it, he said he thought that passing me the ball was pretty much like turning it over to the other team. This conversation was extremely hard on my self-confidence. I felt I was being denied a chance to play and participate fully in the game. I mean, I would be wide open, right underneath the net and still no one passed me the ball. I felt, like, what's the point in even trying. It made me not want to play any more. I might as well have sat underneath my own net and crossed my arms every time my team got the ball and raced down the court, considering how much my team involved me in the offence.

93

I mean, who was he to make that kind of decision? If the coach felt I deserved to be out on the floor then it was only right that my teammates should have respected that and passed me the ball. When this guy refused to pass me the ball the coach should have stepped in and made sure that the team created an atmosphere of inclusion. I felt inadequate and inferior because of the way he treated me, which is ridiculous. The truth is he was a little rat and there was nothing wrong with me. I was exactly where I should be, and if there were more opportunities to compete against other people on the spectrum I would have been able to see that more easily at the time.

Teammates making me feel inferior seems a common theme in many of the teams that I played on. When I was fifteen I played on a soccer team. One of my teammates was having a party and when one of the players asked me whether I was going or not, the guy throwing the party shut him up, because he really didn't want me to come. He and many other players on the team didn't want anything to do with me. They had been nice to me at the beginning of the season but as soon as they saw how weak a player I was, they stopped wanting to have anything to do with me.

One would think that the competitive nature of sports is related to the ignorance of youth and that as people aged they might realize what they were doing was wrong. One might think that people would learn how to relax, since it was clear they were not going to play sports in the highest leagues, and so the only reason to keep participating was for the fun of it. Adults are supposed to be more sensitive towards others' feelings. I had imagined they wouldn't care about winning as much, once their hubris died down in the realization they were not going to play professionally. Amazingly, this was not the case.

In many Beer League tournaments, referred to as such because drinking beer is as important to these men and women as the games themselves, sometimes players organizing a team specifically do not mention upcoming tournaments to some of their teammates. Not because these teammates might have Aspergers and struggle with social skills, but simply because they are not the most talented of players. This action is petty and low, and only Neurotypical people would behave this way. I mean, it is extremely hurtful for people when they find out, which they often do. These are the actions of immature children, not mature grown men.

Another hurtful thing is when the organizers of these teams ask other people who are more talented to substitute for the players not invited. I don't know why these players would go along with this nonsense, but they often collude with the organizers by agreeing to play on these teams. In addition, some of these players are very talented, and then in turn don't pass the puck to the people who brought them in, because they are worried that they will make the team lose. After all, no matter how talented you are, unless you are the very best, you will be the least talented at a higher level. Live by the gun, die by the gun.

This is truly a messed up system. Everyone except for the original victims should just feel ashamed for acting so badly toward other people. I don't think any part of this is healthy. What happened to these individuals' basic humanity? While many of these weaker players may be neurotypical there is a good chance that people on the autism spectrum are not treated any better, because, part of the "condition" means that we generally have poor-hand-eye coordination, and are likely to be on the bottom half of the team, as long as we play in Neurotypical leagues. It is just one more example of Neurotypicals, who many people with Aspergers try to emulate and fit in with, acting badly. Instead of feeling superior, they should be trying to emulate people with Aspergers in working to create a more inclusive environment.

Do not get me wrong. There are a lot of positive things that sports offers people with Aspergers. If playing with Neurotypical people doesn't drive you away, for example, sports can teach the power of teamwork and how to take someone else's perspective. Teamwork is such a valuable skill, it might make someone with Aspergers want to play in a Neurotypical league and in Asperger' tournaments. The truth is, in most workplaces, we are going to have to work with Neurotypicals so we need to learn how they operate, warts and all. How can we still get our mutual goals achieved or even our own goals achieved when their natural mode of thought is more competitive than collaborative?

For example, we might have to play to their ego more and tell them how great they are, if we want to get anything achieved. We might even have to turn certain tasks into a competition, like who can get all these pieces of paper cleaned up first. Sometimes we might even need to frame things in sports terms, like the clock is ticking down and we are fourth down on goal, and everyone is relying on you to get that paper in on time for the victory. Many males only understand things if you can put your points in sports terms. The only reason I know how to talk sports talk and appear inspirational to Neurotypicals is because I played sports myself for many years.

Sports is huge among Neurotypicals, so having played with them gives us a common experience to share, especially when it comes to trying to make conversation with new people with whom we might not have much else to talk about otherwise.

At the same time, it is important that we get opportunities to play with other people on the autism spectrum. It is important to be able to have opportunities to collaborate with people like ourselves, so we can get a sense of belonging. In addition, if you only play with Neurotypicals you might buy into their flawed logic that being the best is the most important quality. You might even start thinking their way, that valuing winning above all is the only way. Then when you get to play with people on the autism spectrum you remember, Nope, it is only one way of thinking and that other things such as camaraderie and fun are just as important.

Finally, let's be honest, playing sports is a lot more fun than going to the gym and just lifting weights, as long as there isn't someone there ruining the experience the whole time. Neurotypicals tend to make even weight lifting or jogging competitive. So if we had our own league or tournaments we would be in much better shape. There are many people who quit sports at a young age because of the pervasive win at all costs mentality, and there is also a high rate of obesity in North America. Coincidence? I think not.

Physical activity has many benefits, including that it helps with mental and emotional health, as it releases endorphins, which make people happier and put them in a better place for making decisions. Therefore, society can hardly afford not to create these leagues and tournaments, when you think about how much money would be saved from absenteeism from work, as well as from medical bills.

I doubt the super competitive nature of Neurotypical sports is going anywhere any time soon. There is simply too much fame, prestige and delusion of grandeur tied in with winning. Therefore, to create a place where people on the spectrum can find a feeling of belonging and not be socially alienated or made to feel worthless for not being the best athlete, I propose the creation of separate leagues and tournaments, designed just for us.

15. Happily Ever After

Like all good parties, things eventually come to an end, including this book. As you read it, there were probably moments of laughter, tears and disagreement. Some people probably quit halfway through, so upset by how I portrayed Neurotypical people. It is often difficult to read hard truths, and the fact that people with Aspergers have better values and qualities, is a very hard truth. It is not easy to have someone point out how the Neurotypical value system is flawed and that it prioritizes some things too highly.

Don't feel bad. Often people with Aspergers can get so caught up in mainstream society that we think the same way you do. I thought winning at sports and life was all important, and was very upset when I realized I was doing poorly. With some distance from the game, however, you can probably agree that it's just ridiculous. It really is.

As I mentioned earlier, there are some good Neurotypical people out there: Mother Teresa, Gandhi or the allies of people with autism. They are the minority, but having read this book, you can take a deep breath and feel satisfied that there is a good chance that you are one of the good ones, too. Hopefully, now that your eyes have been opened to how there is, in fact, a better way of doing things, we can start to change society, so it starts to reflect the utopia people on the autism spectrum would create if Aspies were in control.

98

Now, it definitely will not be easy. The insiders, the beautiful, the elite, and Jenny McCarthy and her anti-vaxxers may try to stop us, but if we move as a united front we shall prevail. I realize that there are additional challenges like getting Aspies together with the good Neurotypicals long enough to make serious plans together. I mean it is hard enough to get Aspies together long enough to come up with dance numbers, like in the hit musical, West Side Story. Nevertheless, we will need to commit many random acts of tolerance in order to overthrow the status quo.

I look forward to working alongside each and every one of you on the hard road ahead, to create a better, a more Aspie oriented society. Just know this, as long as there are people willing to buy my books, I will continue to lead the good fight. It's been great to talk with you.

Adam Schwartz, signing off.

Thank you for reading my book. I hope you enjoyed reading it as much as I enjoyed writing it. I would really appreciate if you recommended it to all your friends or left a review at your favourite retailer.

Cheers

Adam Schwartz

Author Bio

Adam Schwartz is a stand-up comedian on the Autism Spectrum. While it is not quite clear the moment everyone knew he had Aspergers it was a moment to rejoice. Adam is also the founder of Autistic Productions a company dedicated to raising Awareness of Autism through the Auts. He can be contacted through the website for speaking gigs, stand-up comedy shows or just to say hello. Adam resides in Winnipeg, Manitoba.

Made in the USA
Charleston, SC
17 April 2016